COMPUTER PROGRAMMING LANGUAGES
LANGUAGES
A Comparative Introduction

ELLIS HORWOOD SERIES IN COMPUTERS AND THEIR APPLICATIONS
Series Editor: IAN CHIVERS, Consultant to the Monitoring and Assessment Research Centre, London, and formerly Senior Programmer and Analyst, Imperial College of Science and Technology, University of London

Abramsky, S. & Hankin, C.J.	ABSTRACT INTERPRETATION OF DECLARATIVE LANGUAGES
Alexander, H.	FORMALLY-BASED TOOLS AND TECHNIQUES FOR HUMAN–COMPUTER DIALOGUES
Atherton, R.	STRUCTURED PROGRAMMING WITH BBC BASIC
Atherton, R.	STRUCTURED PROGRAMMING WITH COMAL
Baeza-Yates, R.A.	TEXT SEARCHING ALGORITHMS
Bailey, R.	FUNCTIONAL PROGRAMMING WITH HOPE
Barrett, R., Ramsay, A. & Sloman, A.	POP-11
Berztiss, A.	PROGRAMMING WITH GENERATORS
Bharath, R.	COMPUTERS AND GRAPH THEORY
Bishop, P.	FIFTH GENERATION COMPUTERS
Bullinger, H.-J. & Gunzenhauser, H.	SOFTWARE ERGONOMICS
Burns, A.	NEW INFORMATION TECHNOLOGY
Carberry, J.C.	COBOL
Carlini, U. & Villano, U.	TRANSPUTERS AND PARALLEL ARCHITECTURES
Chivers, I.D.	AN INTRODUCTION TO STANDARD PASCAL
Chivers, I.D.	MODULA 2
Chivers, I.D. & Sleighthome, J.	INTERACTIVE FORTRAN 77
Clark, M.W.	PC-PORTABLE FORTRAN
Clark, M.W.	TEX
Colomb, R.	IMPLEMENTING PERSISTENT PROLOG
Cope, T.	COMPUTING USING BASIC
Curth, M.A. & Edelmann, H.	APL
Dahlstrand, I	SOFTWARE PORTABILITY AND STANDARDS
Dongarra, J., Duff, I., Gaffney, P., & McKee, S.	VECTOR AND PARALLEL COMPUTING
Duan-Zheng, X.	COMPUTERS IN SEQUENTIAL MEDICAL TRIALS
Dunne, P.E.	COMPUTABILITY THEORY
Eastlake, J.J.	A STRUCTURED APPROACH TO COMPUTER STRATEGY
Eisenbach, S.	FUNCTIONAL PROGRAMMING
Ellis, D.	MEDICAL COMPUTING AND APPLICATIONS
Ennals, J.R.	ARTIFICIAL INTELLIGENCE
Ennals, J.R.	BEGINNING MICRO-PROLOG
Ennals, J.R., *et al.*	INFORMATION TECHNOLOGY AND EDUCATION
Filipič, B.	PROLOG USER'S HANDBOOK
Ford, N.	COMPUTER PROGRAMMING LANGUAGES
Guariso, G. & Werthner, H.	ENVIRONMENTAL DECISION SUPPORT SYSTEMS
Harland, D.M.	CONCURRENCY AND PROGRAMMING LANGUAGES
Harland, D.M.	POLYMORPHIC PROGRAMMING LANGUAGES
Harland, D.M.	REKURSIV
Harris, D.J.	DEVELOPING DEDICATED DBASE SYSTEMS
Henshall, J. & Shaw, S.	OSI EXPLAINED, 2nd Edition
Hepburn, P.H.	FURTHER PROGRAMMING IN PROLOG
Hepburn, P.H.	PROGRAMMING IN MICRO-PROLOG MADE SIMPLE
Hill, I.D. & Meek, B.L.	PROGRAMMING LANGUAGE STANDARDISATION
Hutchins, W.J.	MACHINE TRANSLATION
Hutchison, D.	FUNDAMENTALS OF COMPUTER LOGIC
Hutchison, D. & Silvester, P.	COMPUTER LOGIC
Koopman, P.	STACK COMPUTERS
Koskimies, K. & Paaki, J.	AUTOMATING LANGUAGE IMPLEMENTATION
Koster, C.H.A.	TOP-DOWN PROGRAMMING WITH ELAN
Last, R.	ARTIFICIAL INTELLIGENCE TECHNIQUES IN LANGUAGE LEARNING
Lester, C.	A PRACTICAL APPROACH TO DATA STRUCTURES
Lucas, R.	DATABASE APPLICATIONS USING PROLOG
Lucas, A.	DESKTOP PUBLISHING
Maddix, F. & Morgan, G.	SYSTEMS SOFTWARE
Matthews, J.L.	FORTH
Millington, D.	SYSTEMS ANALYSIS AND DESIGN FOR COMPUTER APPLICATIONS
Moseley, L.G., Sharp, J.A. & Salenieks, P.	PASCAL IN PRACTICE
Moylan, P.	ASSEMBLY LANGUAGE FOR ENGINEERS
Narayanan, A. & Sharkey, N.E.	AN INTRODUCTION TO LISP
Parrington, N. & Roper, M.	UNDERSTANDING SOFTWARE TESTING
Paterson, A.	OFFICE SYSTEMS
Phillips, C. & Cornelius, B.J.	COMPUTATIONAL NUMERICAL METHODS
Rahtz, S.P.Q.	INFORMATION TECHNOLOGY IN THE HUMANITIES
Ramsden, E.	MICROCOMPUTERS IN EDUCATION 2

Series continued at back of book

COMPUTER PROGRAMMING LANGUAGES
A Comparative Introduction

NEVILLE J. FORD   M.A.(Oxon), M.Sc.
Senior Lecturer in Computer Studies
Chester College of Higher Education

ELLIS HORWOOD
NEW YORK   LONDON   TORONTO   SYDNEY   TOKYO   SINGAPORE

sam

First published in 1990 by
ELLIS HORWOOD LIMITED
Market Cross House, Cooper Street,
Chichester, West Sussex, PO19 1EB, England
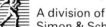
A division of
Simon & Schuster International Group

Printed and bound in Great Britain
by Hartnolls, Bodmin

British Library Cataloguing in Publication Data

Ford, Neville J.
Computer programming languages: a comparative
introduction
1. Microcomputer systems. Programming languages
I. Title
005.26
ISBN 0–13–173071–1 (Student Pbk. Edn.)

Library of Congress Cataloging-in-Publication Data

Ford, Neville J. (Neville John), 1957–
Computer programming languages: a comparative
introduction / Neville J. Ford
p. cm. — (Ellis Horwood series in computers and their
applications)
ISBN 0–13–173071–1 (Student Pbk. Edn.)
1. Programming languages (Electronic computers).
I. Title.   II. Series: Computers and their applications.
QA76.7.F65 1989
005.13—dc20   89–71637
                                                CIP

4-29-91

CONTENTS

Prologue   1

1 Programming Languages   3

    Introduction   3

    What is a programming language?   3

    The Operating System   10

    The Working Environment   10

    Compilers and Interpreters   12

    Languages and Implementations   13

    Standards   13

    Features to look for in a language 14

2 BASIC   17

    Introduction   17

    Background   17

    BASIC Compilers   23

    Turbo BASIC   24

    Who uses BASIC?   24

    BASIC Applications   26

    BASIC's limitations   41

3 Pascal   **49**

    Introduction   49

    Background   49

    Who uses Pascal?   56

    Pascal Applications   60

    Pascal's limitations   74

4 COBOL   **79**

    Introduction   79

    Background   79

    COBOL's facilities   85

    Who uses COBOL?   90

    COBOL Applications   93

    COBOL's limitations   109

5 FORTRAN   **111**

    Introduction   111

    Background   111

    Why FORTRAN?   114

    FORTRAN's facilities   116

    FORTRAN Applications   127

    FORTRAN's limitations   133

6 C   **137**

    Introduction   137

    Background   137

    Programming with C   142

    Routine features of C   146

    Some more advanced features   147

    Who uses C?   159

    C Applications   159

    C's limitations   168

7 Modula-2   **171**

    Introduction   171

    Background   171

    Modula-2's facilities   176

    Separate compilation   186

    Concurrency   189

    Who uses Modula-2?   193

    Modula-2 Applications   193

    Modula-2's limitations   200

8 Prolog   **201**

    Introduction   201

    Background   201

    What does a Prolog program look like?   205

    Who uses Prolog?   211

    Prolog Applications   214

    What is an expert system?   221

    Prolog's limitations   225

9 Exercises   **227**

    Introduction   227

    Questions to ask   227

    Example 1 Company Payroll   229

    Example 2 Personnel Records System   230

    Example 3 Mailing List   232

    Example 4 Health Analysis   232

    Example 5 Health Testing   233

    Example 6 Scientific Data Analysis   233

Epilogue   **235**

    To program or not to program...   235

    Where to from here?   236

Bibliography 237

Language Implementations 240

Index 241

Acknowledgements

I am pleased to acknowledge the assistance I have received from several people in the preparation of the material for this book. I am particularly grateful to my colleague Mark Woodroffe for his advice on the Prolog language, to my wife, Judy, for her general assistance and help with the Pascal language, and to those of my students and colleagues who have identified minor errors in the text. I also received valuable comments from Ian Chivers who read the entire draft of the book.

Neville J. Ford

PROLOGUE

There are many books available which teach you a particular programming language. Each tells you what is good about that language, some also tell you about some of the language's limitations.

This book is not like that. This book is for people who want to know something about lots of programming languages. It has grown out of a lecture course for undergraduates at Chester College which introduces students who have done a little programming before to the wide range of languages which are used in computer applications today.

The book is written on the basis that what most people want to know about a language is 'What is it used for?' and 'Why is it good for that purpose?'. Accordingly there is a chapter on each of seven commonly used languages. Each chapter begins by identifying the language and its main application areas, includes some discussion of the features of the language which make it appropriate for that application area and then gives some real example programs. You will be encouraged, through exercises, to adapt some of the programs to different tasks, and thereby gain a feel for using the different languages.

It is beneficial for you to have access to versions of at least some of the languages for the exercises, but even without this, by the end of the book you will be able decide on suitable choices of language for some realistic case studies. You should also be able to decide on a suitable language to learn next, to suit your interests.

1 Programming Languages

Introduction

This book is about computer programming languages. In the later chapters, we shall discuss seven of the programming languages which are currently used for a variety of applications. In this first chapter, we shall consider what exactly we mean by a programming language, and we shall identify the issues which will be important in our subsequent discussions.

What is a programming language?

Computers obey instructions which are issued to them. In order for the instructions to be understood both by the person who issues them, and by the computer which obeys them, they must be issued in a particular form. The set of instructions and the rules by which they are to be issued and acted upon, forms the basis of the computer language.

The earliest computers were programmed in binary. In other words, each instruction was issued as a series of 1s and 0s, and had a precise meaning. For example:

00010000100

might mean that the computer was to clear its 'accumulator' (workspace where the calculations are performed) in readiness to begin a new calculation.

A computer program is a series of instructions to the computer, which are executed in an appropriate order to perform a particular task. Thus, for these early computers, a program would consist of a series of these instructions written in binary.

Clearly, the issuing of instructions to the computer in binary is a highly specialised task. The instructions available were able to perform only relatively simple tasks, such as adding two numbers together, or moving numbers about from one place to another, and the instructions were not memorable. Writing computer programs was a long job for a specialist computer expert, who might take many hours to find any error, since the purpose of each instruction was far from obvious.

In response to these problems, an improved method of writing programs was introduced, known as assembly language. Assembly language offers the programmer the opportunity to write programs using the same basic set of operations as the previous binary 'machine code' offered, but to write the instructions using mnemonic codes which are far more memorable.

So, for example, the instruction to add two numbers, A and B together, becomes something like

```
ADD A,B
```

There is a problem with assembly programming, however. While the program written in assembly code is much easier for the human programmer to write, understand, and correct, unfortunately the computer does not understand it! What, then is the purpose of writing a program in a language which the computer does not understand?

Alongside the introduction of assembly language, was the introduction of the assembler. An assembler is a program written in machine code, which is able to translate the assembly language instructions into the machine code which they really represent. Each assembly language instruction is an almost exact equivalent of a single machine code instruction. The assembler program consists mainly of reading in the instructions in assembly language, and producing the corresponding machine code instructions.

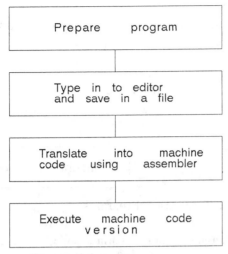

Figure 1.1

Figure 1.1 illustrates the process of writing and translating a program from assembly language into the executable machine code.

The introduction of assembly language in the 1950's provides the key to the subsequent production of 'high-level' computer languages which are the concern of this book. The motive for introducing assembly language was to make programming computers more easy for humans. But assembly language is limited in its facilities since it provides only a little more than those facilities which are already available in machine code. The assembly language programmer has access to machine code instructions and *macros*. A macro offers a single instruction to give a combination of several machine code instructions and provide common requirements. It would be much easier for the programmer to work in a language which provided even more sophisticated facilities. These instructions may each need to be translated into many machine code instructions.

This led to the birth of the earliest 'high level' computer lanuages.

The term high-level language refers to a computer language which is designed to be easy for humans to learn and use. These languages are sometimes known as human-oriented languages. By contrast, a 'low-level' language is one which is close to the machine's own language, and is therefore usually correspondingly harder for humans to use. Typically, we

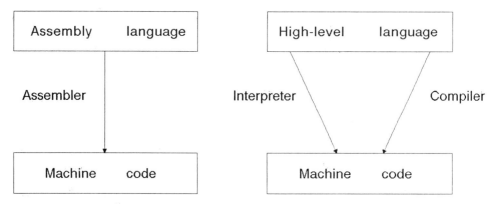

Figure 1.2 Translation Programs

shall refer to assembly language and machine code as being low-level, machine oriented languages, while the other languages which we shall discuss are all 'high-level' languages.

It is natural for us to identify some languages as being 'more high level' than others. These will be the languages which make a particular attempt to provide ease of programming for humans.

All languages, except machine code itself, need to be translated before they may be executed by the computer's processor. Assembly language is translated using an assembler, as described above. High level languages are translated using a 'compiler' or an 'interpreter'. (Figure 1.2).

In order to see more clearly what is involved in the translation process we shall look at a particular simple looping construction and how it would be coded, first using machine level instructions and then using higher level language.

Let us consider how we might repeat a series of instructions 10 times. In machine code, we would typically do this by using a 'JUMP' instruction, in a construction like this:

```
PUT 10 INTO A
START SUBTRACT 1 FROM A
<do the other things we want to repeat>
JUMP TO START IF A IS NOT 0
```

If we were working in a high level language, it is very unlikely that we would have to actually set up the 'loop' in this way. Instead, we would be provided with some sort of construction to do this for us. For example, in BASIC, we might write the program section like this:

```
FOR A = 1 TO 10
<do the things we want to repeat>
NEXT A
```

or in Pascal, we might write:

```
for a:=1 to 10 do
begin
<do the thing we want to repeat>
end;
```

In each case, the high level language's looping construction is replaced by several machine code instructions when the program is translated. The high level language is easier for the programmer to write, and gives a clearer indication of what the section of program is doing.

So far, we have identified computer programming languages as providing a convenient way to give a series of instructions to the computer processor, but that is not their only function. A second, very important function, is the language's ability to handle memory and allocate it for the use of a program.

Once again, it is probably easiest to see what is going on if we consider what is required of the programmer who works in machine code. The memory of the computer can be thought of as a series of boxes, and each box has an address (figure 1.3). For the programmer using machine code, the use to which each box is to be put must be explicitly determined and specified. The programmer must decide which boxes are to be allocated for the actual instructions to be stored, and which are to be used for data. Each storage location in memory can take a binary number of a predetermined length (typically 8, 16 or 32 bits). Each one of these binary numbers may be used to store either program instructions or data. The programmer in machine code must be careful to ensure that data never occupies the same location as a program instruction, since the processor will translate the binary number contained in any memory location according to the context. This dual purpose nature of memory locations has the advantage that the same area of memory

Address	Contents
1	00001011
2	10110001
3	11001001
4	01010110
5	11111001
6	11011101
7	01011101
8	10111010

Figure 1.3 Each memory location has an address and contains a binary number which can be either data or an instruction.

may be used for large amounts of data for a small program or for a larger program which requires less data storage. The idea is known as 'Von Neuman's stored program concept'.

Assembly language offers the programmer the advantage of being able to specify whereabouts in the memory a particular program and its data should start (i.e. the address of the first memory location used) and then the assembler will take account of where to put each program instruction and each item of data. The programmer is able to refer to any item of data and any particular instruction by means of a symbol which is translated by the assembler into the actual address. This relieves the programmer of the responsibility of keeping such careful control over the memory.

High level languages typically take all the responsibility away from the programmer, who will be unaware of where in the memory either the program or the data is stored. The use of variable names allows for the references to particular data items. Labels, named procedures and subroutines and line numbers allow reference to be made to particular parts of the program. These references are translated by the compiler or interpreter into the addresses in memory where the particular data or instruction is held. More complex types of data may also become available when a high level language is in use. For example, we may be able to store lists or arrays of similar types of data, or strings of characters, or numbers to a particularly high degree of accuracy.

The third function of the programming language is the way in which it gives the programmer facilities to access the hardware which is part of the computer system. Figure 1.4 illustrates a typical computer system. If programming in machine code, the programmer would need to address the various items of hardware at machine level in order to operate them. So, for example, in order to display a message on the computer screen, the user would need to know which location in the memory corresponded to the particular location on the screen and insert the necessary codes into those locations. Similarly, to send output to the printer, the programmer would need to know how to address the printer at the hardware level. This would typically involve sending data to the numbered port which the 'operating system' had allocated as being the channel to which the printer output had been connected.

For the high level language programmer, these details are not usually relevant, since most programming languages will provide special instructions to send output to the screen or the printer, or perhaps to collect data from a computer input port. However, the routines provided within the languages can sometimes prove insufficiently flexible for a particular application, and it then becomes the programmer's job to find a way of using the lower level instructions directly. Some languages give the

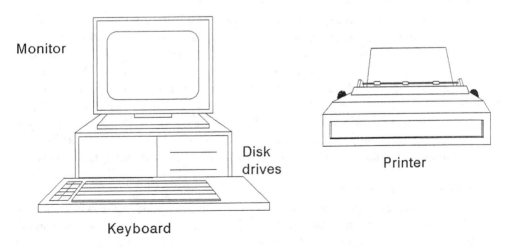

Figure 1.4 The components of a typical small computer system

programmer easy access to these 'low level' facilities, and we shall identify these later. Some other high level languages 'protect' their users from these 'difficult' areas.

The operating system

The user of any modern computer system will face two sets of commands. The programming language will provide one set of these, and the operating system provides the other.

The operating system is a program which is loaded each time the computer is turned on, and continues to run until the computer is closed down. It provides the set of instructions which the programmer will need to control the operation of the computer, for example to log in, to display directory information, to load a file or program, and to run a program. The operating system also has responsibility for a number of other functions, many of which will not be apparent to the individual user. For example, the operating system on a large computer installation might monitor which users are currently entitled to large amounts of processor time, and which should be given a reduced allocation. Additionally, the amount of disk and memory space used by each user will be monitored and controlled. The appropriate peripherals for a particular user will be allocated by the operating system, which will probably also provide facilities for an individual to override the default settings if he desires to do so.

It is the operating system program which provides the facilities whereby communication may be initiated and continued with the peripherals. It is therefore necessary for the low-level language programmer to know the necessary operating system codes to address the ports to which the peripherals are connected. The high level programmer, who is working in a computer language which is provided for the particular operating system in use, will usually find that the links to the operating system are already established, and that therefore it is possible to communicate with peripherals using high-level programming instructions.

The working environment

The programmer will need to work within some environment which gives access to instructions allowing programs to be input, saved, loaded, translated and executed. The exact form of this working environment varies.

On most older systems the programmer works at the operating system level. He calls, from the operating system, on the 'editor', a program rather like a wordprocessor which allows the program to be typed in and altered, and on the compiler or interpreter, which translates the code. In the case of a compiler, the programmer will need to issue a separate instruction to actually run the translated version, whereas with an interpreter, this will be automatic. (See below for more details).

The series of steps which must be taken to develop a new program in one of these older systems would typically be something like this:

1) Invoke the editor to type in the program

2) Exit from the editor and save the program in a file

3) Invoke the translation program and take note of errors

4) Reload the editor with the program and make changes as appropriate to correct errors

5) Repeat 3 and 4 to remove all errors until compilation is successful

6) Execute translated program, as appropriate.

Some languages, notably BASIC, have, from the earliest versions, sought to provide programmers with a 'friendlier' development environment, which avoids the repeated switching between the editor and the compiler/interpreter via the operating system. This has often been accomplished by incorporating the operating system commands, the editor and an interpreter within a single package. (See chapter 2 for more details of this approach).

More recent developments by some suppliers of high level languages have reacted to the demand from users for languages to be provided in a form which is both easier to use and faster to move between the editor and the compiler. These 'integrated development environments' are becoming increasingly popular, and it is likely that users of microcomputer language implementations will find these readily available. The only problem with such systems can be that they may have the editor and compiler co-resident in the memory at any given instant and therefore may take up rather a lot of memory, which thereby limits the amount of memory available for the source and object code versions of the program. (Source code is the program as typed in, prior to translation, and object code is the translated version of the program which the compiler produces.) Better implementations overcome these memory constraints by the use of *overlays* and interchange parts of the system between disk and memory while in use.

Compilers and Interpreters

We have referred already to the use of translation programs to convert the high level computer programming language into the executable machine code which the computer processor can 'understand'. While there is only one task to perform, there are two distinct methods of doing this:

Compilers take the entire source code program and convert it into object code. This means that the entire program is translated in one go and resaved in its converted form. The translated object code is then *linked* and finally run. There is no possibility of finding any errors of syntax (grammar) when the program is run, since these would have been shown up by the compiler at the translation stage. It is also the case that because the translation is undertaken in advance, compiled programs run quickly, when compared to interpreted programs. There is no need to recompile a program once compiled, it may be run repeatedly.

There may be some space disadvantages in using a compiler since we need to find space to accommodate both the source and object files.

Interpreters take the program one statement at a time and translate and execute the single statement before going on to the next. This means that the translation and execution phases happen together and not separately as in the case of the compiler. The main advantage of the interpreter is that the environment is often better suited to debugging programs than the compiler environment and is generally easier to use.

Interpreters suffer from poorer execution speeds than their compiler competitors, since the code must be translated each time it is executed. This speed deterioration is particularly marked in the case of programs where a single instruction is repeated several times, since it must be translated each time by the interpreter whereas the compiler would only translate it once.

Languages and Implementations

One of the questions which this book seeks to answer is which language should be chosen for a particular application. However, selecting an appropriate language is not the only task. Equally important is the selection of a suitable 'implementation' of the language selected.

Each software manufacturer which chooses to distribute a language must select:

1) The hardware which is to be supported, and an appropriate underlying operating system for the chosen hardware.

2) The precise version of the language which will be implemented: which commands will be included, which will be excluded, whether any additions to the usual language specifications are desirable, and whether to offer any standard applications ready written for adaptation. These might be offered in the form of library programs.

3) The working environment: interpreter or compiler, integrated environment or 'traditional' working style.

The decisions made here will determine how acceptable to the programmers in the market-place the particular version of the programming language on offer will be.

For example, Pascal might seem a fairly unlikely choice of language for many mainstream applications packages for microcomputers, but Borland's Turbo Pascal was an attractive implementation at a very attractive price when it was released. The result was that Turbo Pascal became the accepted development language for many applications.

Standards

One question which we shall consider when looking at each language, is the extent to which the language has an agreed standard which is enforced in a recognised way.

One may question whether it is really important for a language implementation to adhere rigidly to a particular standard. The advantages of it doing so are:

1) The programs written which conform to the standard are 'portable' and therefore the programs are not tied to a particular hardware set-up. The value of the programs written in a language may far exceed the actual cost of both the hardware configuration and the language compilers.

2) It is possible to recruit experienced programmers to fill vacancies.

3) It is possible to buy in programs which have been written by

others using the same standard version and also library procedures and routines.

The disadvantage of standards can be that they are slow to adapt to newer hardware and newer applications and may cause languages to become out-of-date, which may encourage implementors to add their own extensions.

Most standards for language conformity are issued by either the American standards authority (ANSI) or the International Standards Organisation (ISO). Individual countries also have their own standards authorites which make a contribution (eg BSI in Britain and DIN in Germany). Naturally, it takes time for the approved standard to be established for newer languages. Equally important to establishing the standard is the instigation of approved methods for testing conformance to the standard. A standard which is not adequately checked is little better than no standard at all.

Typically a series of programs (a 'validation suite') are prepared by the standards organisation, who then attempt to run those programs on 'standard' implementations of the language. It is then possible to establish by how far the so-called conformist language deviates from the true standard.

Features to look for in a language

Apart from implementation features, which inevitably vary between implementations of the same language, we shall be trying to identify the features of programming languages which make them particularly suited to specific applications.

We shall be considering some 'general purpose' computer languages alongside some which are particularly designed for certain types of application. Some people would favour the introduction of a single language which would be used for all possible applications, but there would be disadvantages in that:

1) Such a language would be very large and difficult to learn fully, and hard to implement on small computers

2) The language would inevitably have features which made programming particular applications less efficient than using a special-purpose language.

In order to illustrate more clearly the need for special-purpose computer languages, we may draw an example from natural languages. In order to describe different types of snow adequately, Eskimos have a great many more words than the English language provides. This is because they have more different features of the snow which they want to be able to express.

In a similar way, a specialised file-handling computer programming language might provide lots of ways of describing a file, and a specialised numerical processing language might offer lots of ways of describing exactly the sort of number which is required for a particular task.

So, one of the questions which we shall be considering is 'in what ways may data be described, manipulated and stored,' since this determines the types of application which are suited to coding in the particular language.

Another very important issue concerns the type of control structures which the language offers. Earlier in the chapter, we were able to see how much easier it was to describe a repetition in a high level language by means of a looping construction than it was in machine code when we needed to use explicit jumps to a particular address. There are other control structures which we shall meet which allow us to write 'well structured' programs. These include the facility to give a section of the program a name and call it as a named procedure or subroutine. This enhances the readability of the program and also provides an easy way to re-use a section of program in a number of different places within a program and keep the total length of the code to a minimum. The provision of library routines and externally compiled procedures can also increase the power and flexibility of the language and are another feature which we shall look out for.

Don't Panic!

This is the end of the introductory chapter. We have covered a lot of ground in an attempt to set the scene for the later work. If some of this has been unfamiliar, and you are worrying about the later content, then don't panic. The later chapters contain lots of example programs and lots of practical work to do. If you then come back to this chapter at the end, you will almost certainly find it quite straightforward.

2 BASIC

Introduction

The first specific language which we shall consider is BASIC. BASIC is an old language which has become particularly commonly used recently for programming smaller microcomputer systems.

Background

The programming language BASIC (Beginners' All-purpose Symbolic Instruction Code) was developed in 1964 at Dartmouth College, Hanover, New Hampshire, USA. Its invention was motivated by the desire to have available a programming language which would be simpler to learn than FORTRAN, and which would provide students with a good introduction to programming in readiness to learn to use FORTRAN later.

The earliest use of BASIC was therefore in Education, but its use spread to other areas as people discovered that BASIC could be used, not only for an introduction before learning to program in another language, but also as an applications programming language in its own right. BASIC was soon seen as a language which offered programmers many of the facilities of FORTRAN for the writing of routine programs, and the added advantage of easier program development and a rather more user-friendly syntax. BASIC only really loses out to FORTRAN when the more advanced features of the FORTRAN language are required. For mathematicians and some scientists, most applications programs do need these advanced features of the language, but for many users, BASIC performs more than adequately.

Although designed originally as a substitute for FORTRAN, BASIC has always aimed to be a general purpose language. Therefore the range of facilities on offer have made it a reasonable choice of language for a wide range of programming tasks, although specialised languages would often provide a neater solution.

BASIC has an interesting history, since it was much less often used early in its life and its use has become significantly greater more recently. The really 'serious' computer applications of the 1960's and 1970's were not written in BASIC. Software developers chose larger and more sophisticated languages which were better suited to the particular application in hand. As a result, the number of BASIC users was, for a long time, substantially smaller than the number of users of the language COBOL, for example.

The advent of the microcomputer, and the desire among manufacturers of these small computer systems for a language which was accessible to the beginner, and easy to implement on a small scale led most hardware manufacturers to adopt BASIC as the preferred language. The large-scale success of the microcomputer has led to the increasing use of computer languages in general, and because it is often the language provided with a computer as standard, of BASIC in particular.

It is interesting at this point to consider the question: "Why was BASIC an attractive choice for microcomputer manufacturers looking for a high-level language for their hardware?"

1) BASIC is an interpretive language.

Almost all implementations of the BASIC language use an interpreter rather than a compiler. The language is designed in such a way that it works particularly well in an interpreted implementation, and in a small computer system, where memory is particularly tight, the use of an interpreter rather than a compiler is beneficial.

The reason for this is fairly obvious: when a compiled language is used, we take the entire source code and translate it into the executable object code and then 'run' the object code. With an interpreter, on the other hand, only one line of the program at a time is translated and therefore it is necessary only to store the source code and the translation of one line. The saving in memory of this approach can be very large.

2) BASIC is an attractive name for a language which needs to attract the masses to buy computers.

Certainly the manufacturers of computers had alternative languages available to them, some of which could have been implemented using an interpreter if necessary, but the description of the computer language as being designed for 'beginners' and being very 'basic' was attractive to those hoping to find a large market for their computers.

3) BASIC is a system, not just a language.

The user of a computer system who wishes to develop programs needs to learn two sets of instructions. The computer's 'operating system' provides the means for communication with the hardware. Commands to load a particular file into RAM, to save the contents of RAM to a file, and to enter the 'editor' are all operating systems commands. These are distinct from the programming language commands which instruct the computer what to do while the program is actually executing.

For users of most computer languages, there is a rigid demarcation between, on the one hand, the operating system commands, which must be issued at the operating system prompt, and the programming language's statements. This causes problems to the beginner. Different types of instruction are needed at different times. Using operating instructions within a computer program is not allowed, and neither must computer programming statements be addressed to the operating system.

The designers of the BASIC language sought to overcome this problem by designing the BASIC environment as a 'system' rather than just as a language in the normal sense of the word. This BASIC system contains its own editor and set of operating system commands. These commands form a part of the language, and may therefore be used within programs if this is desired. Conversely, the programming language commands may be used outside of a program (the so-called 'direct' mode) in which case they are executed immediately.

The effect of this approach is that the BASIC programmer begins the session by entering the BASIC environment (which may be automatic, particularly with smaller microcomputers) and thereafter issues BASIC commands, including the provided BASIC operating system commands.

Figure 2.1 shows a typical sample dialogue for a BASIC programmer using a BASIC system. In the dialogue, the words NEW, LIST, RUN and SAVE are all operating system commands, while the lines typed in beginning with line numbers are instructions to the editor to add these instructions to the stored program. The computer responds to operating system instructions with the word 'Ready'.

```
NEW
Ready
10 REM EXAMPLE PROGRAM
20 PRINT "Hello, what's your name"
30 INPUT NAME$
40 PRINT "That's a nice name"
LIST
10 REM EXAMPLE PROGRAM
20 PRINT "Hello, what's your name"
30 INPUT NAME$
40 PRINT "That's a nice name"
Ready
RUN
Hello, what's your name
? FRED
That's a nice name
Ready
```

Figure 2.1 A sample dialogue with an interactive BASIC system.

For the designers of smaller microcomputers, the use of BASIC allowed for the easy incorporation of operating system commands in this way within the same environment as the language instructions. It was unnecessary for them to provide separate operating system, editor, and run-time environments, and this saved on space, and allowed for the provision of all the language and operating system commands on a single ROM chip in many cases.

4) BASIC is versatile

a) Hardware versatility

In some respects, the statement 'BASIC is versatile' is the positive side of the statement 'BASIC is non-standard'. As an early language which has continued in use through changes in the underlying hardware, it is unsurprising to find that BASIC has adapted from its earliest form. Unfortunately, unlike other languages which have undergone similar metamorphoses, BASIC has been allowed to change in an uncontrolled way. There is therefore wide disparity between different software supplier's implementations of the language. There are certain common features which exist in almost all BASIC implementations, but these are really rather few.

This non-standardisation has a positive side as well as a negative one. We shall see later how slow some languages are forced to be to react to changes in hardware. When a rigid standard is imposed, it is necessary to have the standard revised to meet new situations, and this is time-consuming. Manufacturers faced with changes in hardware suffer no such inhibitions where BASIC is concerned and freely adapt the language by adding commands to suit. Naturally the portability of programs (and programmers!) between different implementations of BASIC suffers as a result of this lack of standardisation, but the relative standardisation of the operating system commands within the BASIC environment between different implementations offers some compensation for having to adapt to new language instructions.

There have been some attempts at standardisation of the BASIC language, but most have been related to giving a specification to a very restricted range of instructions which all BASICs should include. The idea is, that programmers who desire a portable program should then confine themselves to the use of the commands on this restrictive list.

b) Software versatility

BASIC is a general purpose language, and therefore suits the production of computer software for a wide range of application areas. For a manufacturer to specify a particular language as the basis for a micro-computer, he needs to be convinced that the language is sufficiently versatile to allow for all the software demanded by users to be developed. BASIC has turned out to be a reasonably good choice, because it is versatile and is also usually designed to provide fairly ready access to machine code routines when the BASIC language falls down in an application.

Despite all these advantages, BASIC has rather a bad image among many within the computer industry. It is instructive to consider why this should be, particularly since it is the first language met by many entrants to the industry:

1) BASIC is non-standard.

The statement, 'this person has a full knowledge of BASIC programming' is meaningless. Since implementations of the language vary in their range of facilities by several hundred percent, it is impossible to distinguish what is meant by a *full knowledge* of the language.

2) BASIC is often unstructured.

BASIC was designed well before the days when structured programming became the normal approved method. The result is that, while most modern implementations of the language do offer such constructions as REPEAT...UNTIL or WHILE..., this is by no means universal. Many text books widely used in teaching the language adopt earlier 'badly structured' approaches and introduce the reader to bad habits which will need to be overcome before he may be successful as a programmer in the present climate.

3) BASIC is 'peculiar'

Almost all languages currently used are implemented by means of a compiler. Therefore, users of any of these languages become familiar with the use of the computer's operating system and the use of the editor to prepare code for compilation. The steps required in converting to another language therefore consist of learning the new language's syntax. Unfortunately, from this point of view, the average BASIC programmer will have had no need to interact separately with an editor, a compiler and the operating system, and therefore will need to become aware of a whole new set of techniques when transferring to a compiled language. There can be the additional problem that many BASIC programmers become confused over the distinction between the operating system commands and the BASIC language commands, since all may be used interchangeably. This may cause serious problems in transferring to a new language.

One major difficulty is the size of the problem which may be solved satisfactorily using BASIC. For smaller problems BASIC is easy to learn and very satisfactory, but it is difficult to do large-scale development well. For the casual programmer, BASIC is therefore a good choice, but for the serious programmer it is much less appropriate.

Some academics would go as far as to say that they would prefer to teach a student with no previous experience of programming at all, rather than one who has previously been taught BASIC, but to say this is unfair. Most academics agree that a language such as Pascal makes a better introduction to programming than BASIC, but it is certainly the case that poorly written programs may be developed using Pascal, just as they can be using BASIC. Conversely, well written BASIC programs may be compared favourably with the best Pascal programs. The problem lies more in the way that the tools are used than in the tools themselves. It is true that a much larger proportion of BASIC programs are badly written than are Pascal programs. But with the correct guidance, well written BASIC programs are possible, so long as a sufficiently modern and well structured version of the language is selected.

BASIC Compilers

Almost all of the above is written assuming that a BASIC system will be implemented using an Interpreter. BASIC compilers also exist, but are uncommon. The advantage of a BASIC compiler is that it provides code which executes much more quickly than would the corresponding interpreter. Compilers are not usually used for BASIC program development, largely because the main advantage of the language lies in the ease of the BASIC system approach and if a compiler is to be used, then a more application specific language may be preferred. Often compilers follow closely the implementation of a commonly used interpreter, and offer the opportunity to develop the program using the interpreter and then optimise the execution speed through the use of the compiler.

Turbo BASIC

Turbo BASIC provides a compiler within an integrated programming development environment, which combines many of the advantages of the interpreter with the speed of execution associated with a compiler. This is one of the newer approaches to high level programming which makes optimum use of the computer facilities to make life easier for the programmer.

Who Uses BASIC?

There are several types of programmer who work using BASIC.

1) The hobbyist programmer.

By far the largest of these groups is comprised of the hobbyist computer users who purchased a microcomputer and received a BASIC system 'free' with the hardware. These users are sometimes unaware of the availability of alternative languages, or see no reason to buy an alternative when BASIC seems perfectly well suited to their purposes.

The types of programming projects undertaken by such users are as diverse as the interests of the users themselves, and they range from the most trivial interactive programs which merely carry on a conversation through a series of questions, to sophisticated database packages and games programs which have elaborate use of graphics.

The versatility of the particular implementations of BASIC provided is the key to the language's success for these users. They are not motivated to seek alternative languages, because the BASIC language already available offers the capacity to perform all the processing which they require. Easy interfacing to machine code routines fills any gaps which might otherwise exist.

One area which appeals to hobbyist programmers, and is particularly unsuited to most of the rival languages is Graphics. Most hobbyists are keen to write programs which look good, and many are interested in writing computer games. Implementations of languages such as Pascal and C, both of which we shall discuss later, attempt to conform to a standard, which takes no account of the inevitably machine dependent graphics systems. It is therefore rather more difficult for suppliers of compilers in these languages to provide a good range of graphics routines while continuing to conform to the language's specification. BASIC implementors often take full advantage of the graphics facilities on offer, and make it easier for these games programs to be developed by the inexperienced programmer. Modern microcomputers, especially 16-bit machines offer good Musical ability. This is similarly machine-dependent and therefore well-suited to the BASIC language.

Note: It is important to realise here the significance of the term *inexperienced* in the paragraph above. Languages such as C can provide professional programmers with a very acceptable development environment for graphical applications, which will execute far more rapidly and effectively than their counterparts developed in BASIC. However this requires the development and use of specialised library routines (see chapter 6).

2) The occasional computer user.

For those whose use of computer programs is only occasional, and who desire the flexibility of an all-purpose language, BASIC is an ideal choice. The effort involved in learning the language is less than for many of its competitors, and provided that the application does not require very substantial processing, the speed disadvantage of running an interpreted language will go unnoticed.

3) Commercial users.

There are a surprising number of commercial users of BASIC. They are motivated by the desire to continue to maintain existing programs which have been developed in BASIC for some reason, and by the ready availability of a large number of programmers who are proficient in using BASIC. BASIC can also allow rapid development of programs and quite fast execution on the better BASIC implementations. These factors keep the cost of employing BASIC programmers lower than the comparable cost for other languages. However for the reasons which we identified earlier it may be that programmers experienced in BASIC will adapt to their work less rapidly than those trained in the use of other languages and will produce programs which are less well written and harder to maintain.

4) Educational users.

Many of the earlier computers used in schools were most satisfactorily programmed using BASIC. The majority of educational software developed during the 1980's has therefore been developed entirely in BASIC or mainly in BASIC with some machine code. Although the newer computers would be, perhaps, more appropriately programmed using an alternative language, there is a large reservoir of BASIC programmers, both among teachers involved in instruction of computer programmers, and among those who develop educational software, who most naturally turn to the BASIC language.

BASIC Applications

In this section, we shall consider two different types of example. First, we shall look at some simple applications and their implementations in BASIC. We shall consider how different implementations of the language affect how a particular problem would be solved, and we also consider those standard features of BASIC which are particularly powerful. Then later, we shall identify some particular implementations of BASIC which provide some very useful and unusual features.

Example 1

In this first example, we consider the problem of setting up a menu-driven program which provides a series of options, each of which results in a different action being undertaken.

Figure 2.2 illustrates the main menu of the application, which gives the user the choice of selecting between different shapes. According to which shape has been selected, a second screen such as that illustrated in figure 2.3 allows the user to give the values of certain dimensions so that the area of the figure may be calculated by the computer.

```
Select     the     required     shape

1.     Square

2.     Triangle

3.     Rectangle

               ?
```

Figure 2.2 A simple menu screen

This simple application may be implemented in the program listed in figure 2.4. This particular program is written on the assumption that only the most rudimentary of control structures are provided by the particular version of BASIC in use. The IF..THEN..GOTO statement provides the basis for branching in this example, which is fairly typical of the type of program written in early BASIC versions.

You   selected   a   square

Please   type   in   the   length
of   a   side   of   the   square:

                ? 2

The   area   is   4   square   units

Figure 2.3   The 'square' data-entry screen

```
10 REM FIGURE 2.4
20 CLS
30 PRINT
40 PRINT "Select the required shape"
50 PRINT
60 PRINT "1 Square"
70 PRINT
80 PRINT "2 Triangle"
90 PRINT
100 PRINT "3 Rectangle"
110 PRINT
120 PRINT " ";
130 INPUT X
140 IF X = 1 THEN GOTO 200
150 IF X = 2 THEN GOTO 400
160 IF X = 3 THEN GOTO 700
170 GOTO 20
```

```
200 REM SQUARE
210 CLS
220 PRINT
230 PRINT "You selected a square"
240 PRINT
250 PRINT
260 PRINT "Please type in the length"
270 PRINT "of a side of the square"
280 PRINT
290 PRINT " ";
300 INPUT Y
310 PRINT
320 PRINT "The area is "; Y*Y
330 STOP

400 REM TRIANGLE
410 CLS
420 PRINT
430 PRINT "You selected a triangle"
440 PRINT
450 PRINT
460 PRINT "Please type in the length"
470 PRINT "of the base of the triangle"
480 PRINT
490 PRINT " ";
500 INPUT Y
510 PRINT
530 PRINT "Please type in the length"
```

```
540 PRINT "of the height of the triangle"
550 PRINT
560 PRINT " ";
570 INPUT Z
580 PRINT
590 PRINT "The area of the triangle is "; Y*Z/2
600 STOP

700 REM RECTANGLE
710 CLS
720 PRINT
730 PRINT "You selected a rectangle"
740 PRINT
750 PRINT
760 PRINT "Please type in the length"
770 PRINT "of the base of the rectangle"
780 PRINT
790 PRINT " ";
800 INPUT Y
810 PRINT
830 PRINT "Please type in the length"
840 PRINT "of the height of the rectangle"
850 PRINT
860 PRINT " ";
870 INPUT Z
880 PRINT
890 PRINT "The area of the rectangle is "; Y*Z
900 STOP
```
Figure 2.4

More modern BASICs often allow the user to write procedures and to include an ELSE clause within the IF statement. Accordingly, figure 2.5 lists an alternative version of the program which uses these more sophisticated controls. It is clear to any reader that the latter program is the more readable, and the better designed, although the earlier version is slightly shorter. However, the second version is less portable, since it assumes:

a) the existence of the ELSE clause in the IF statement. This is commonly included, but is by no means universal.

b) the existence of procedures called in a particular way; three versions of BASIC currently widely used on microcomputers use the following three different ways of calling the named procedure 'Fred':

```
CALL FRED

FRED

PROCEDURE FRED
```

Clearly, all three versions of the language are providing the same facility, but since they provide it in a different way, the program may not be instantly transported from the one version to another. It is, however, the case that the earlier version of the program would run on almost any implementation of BASIC.

```
10 REM FIGURE 2.5

20 CLS

30 PRINT

40 PRINT "Select the required shape"

50 PRINT

60 PRINT "1 Square"

70 PRINT

80 PRINT "2 Triangle"

90 PRINT

100 PRINT "3 Rectangle"
```

```
110 PRINT
120 PRINT " ";
130 INPUT X
140 IF X = 1 THEN CALL SQUARE ELSE IF X = 2 THEN CALL
TRIANGLE ELSE IF X = 3 THEN CALL RECTANGLE
150 END

200 SUB SQUARE
210 CLS
220 PRINT
230 PRINT "You selected a square"
240 PRINT
250 PRINT
260 PRINT "Please type in the length"
270 PRINT "of a side of the square"
280 PRINT
290 PRINT " ";
300 INPUT Y
310 PRINT
320 PRINT "The area is "; Y*Y
330 END SUB

400 SUB TRIANGLE
410 CLS
420 PRINT
430 PRINT "You selected a triangle"
440 PRINT
450 PRINT
460 PRINT "Please type in the length"
```

```
470 PRINT "of the base of the triangle"
480 PRINT
490 PRINT " ";
500 INPUT Y
510 PRINT
530 PRINT "Please type in the length"
540 PRINT "of the height of the triangle"
550 PRINT
560 PRINT " ";
570 INPUT Z
580 PRINT
590 PRINT "The area of the triangle is "; Y*Z/2
600 END SUB

700 SUB RECTANGLE
710 CLS
720 PRINT
730 PRINT "You selected a rectangle"
740 PRINT
750 PRINT
760 PRINT "Please type in the length"
770 PRINT "of the base of the rectangle"
780 PRINT
790 PRINT " ";
800 INPUT Y
810 PRINT
830 PRINT "Please type in the length"
840 PRINT "of the height of the rectangle"
850 PRINT
```

```
860 PRINT " ";
870 INPUT Z
880 PRINT
890 PRINT "The area of the rectangle is "; Y*Z
900 END SUB
```

Figure 2.5

Exercise 2.6 Try to find out how to draw shapes in your version of BASIC, if it allows the use of graphics. You should then adapt the programs given above to allow the choice of a particular shape to produce an illustration of the selected shape. If you succeed with this, then try including a second menu which offers a choice of colour for the illustration.

Example 2

The second example program illustrates something rather interesting about the way in which BASIC handles its storage of variables. Many computer languages insist that all the variables which are to be used for storage during the running of a program are 'declared' at the beginning of a program so that the necessary memory may be allocated to them in advance. This is the case, for example, when programming in Pascal (see chapter 3). BASIC, however, imposes no such restriction, and simply allocates memory to a variable when the variable is first encountered.

This latter approach is closely tied to BASIC's usual implementation which uses an interpreter, since the interpreter does not encounter the line of code which refers to a particular variable until it actually tries to execute it, but the feature is nevertheless normally retained in BASICs which are implemented by means of a compiler.

A programmer developing a program may often find it convenient to introduce a new variable at will, without having to worry about changing the earlier part of the program to take account of it. This may assist the rapid development of small-scale systems, but this ill-disciplined type of program development is not to be encouraged for larger projects. On the other hand, it may be that for certain applications, the ability to use memory for data only when it is actually encountered is beneficial.

Figure 2.7 shows a BASIC program which allows the input of a class list, which is stored in the array A$(). The first question asks for the necessary information to decide how big the array needs to be, and this is then used in the DIMension statement which actually allocates the storage for the array. The corresponding Pascal code is shown in figure 2.8, and illustrates how the storage must be allocated in advance, and will be rather wasteful to avoid having to abort the program run too frequently if the size of the class should exceed the size of the array allocated.

```
10 REM PROGRAM 2.7
20 REM STORES AN ARRAY OF NAMES
30 CLS
40 PRINT "How many children are there in the class"
50 INPUT C
60 DIM A$(C)
70 FOR I = 1 TO C
80 PRINT "TYPE IN NAME NUMBER ";I
90 INPUT A$(I)
100 NEXT I
```

Figure 2.7 BASIC program to read in a list of variable length

```
program figure2point8(input,output);
const
maxclasssize = 30;
type
name = packed array[1..20] of char;
var
classsize,i : integer;
classlist : array[1..maxclasssize] of name;
begin
writeln('Type in class size');
```

```
readln(classsize);
if classsize > maxclasssize then
  writeln('Sorry, too big')
else
  begin
  for i := 1 to classsize do
      begin
      writeln('Type in name ',i);
      readinstring(classlist[i]);
      {readinstring is a procedure which will need to
      be written, see chapter 3}
      end
  end
end.
```

Figure 2.8 The Pascal program corresponding to the BASIC program in figure 2.7

We might meet another application where the sizes of two arrays are related. For example, array A might contain the dimensions of vacant building plots on a new residential developement, while array B$ contains the names of the occupants of the finished houses. Obviously the total number of entries in these two arrays is equal to the total number of plots on the estate, but the number of entries in each will vary as the estate is built. It could be that the computer has insufficient memory to make the Pascal declarations:

```
const plots = 5000;
type names = packed array[1..50] of char;
dimensions = array[1..2] of integer;
var a: array[1..plots] of names;
b: array[1..plots] of dimensions;
```

whereas the BASIC code:

```
PLOTS = 5000
INPUT VACANT
OCCUPIED = PLOTS - VACANT
DIM A$(OCCUPIED)
DIM B(VACANT,2)
```

might succeed because the total size of the two arrays need only be 5000, rather than the 5000 size of each in the Pascal program.

Exercise 2.9 Try to write a program which stores a list of 25 names in an array of strings. Keep the program to extend later.

Example 3

Following on from example 2, another feature of BASIC is its ability to handle strings of various lengths, without the need for the programmer to specify the length of the string, in characters, in advance.

The language is, therefore, able to offer some sophisticated string handling functions for concatenation and splitting of strings. Figure 2.10 shows an example on-screen dialogue which illustrates how these string functions may be used to give a friendly conversation between the computer and a user. The corresponding BASIC code is given in figure 2.11.

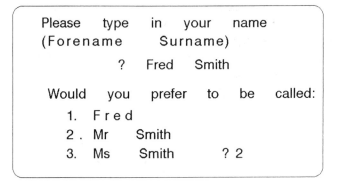

Figure 2.10

```
10 REM PROGRAM 2.11
20 REM PROGRAM TO CHECK ON CORRECT METHOD OF ADDRESS
30 CLS
40 PRINT
50 PRINT "Please type in your name"
60 PRINT " (Forename Surname)"
70 INPUT N$
80 I=0
90 I=I+1
100 IF MID$(N$,I,1) <> " " THEN GOTO 90
110 F$ = LEFT$(N$,I-1)
120 S$ = RIGHT$(N$,LEN(N$)-I)
130 PRINT "Would you prefer to be called:"
140 PRINT "1. ";F$
150 PRINT "2. Mr ";S$
160 PRINT "3. Ms ";S$;" ";
170 INPUT A
```

Figure 2.11

The cleverness of this particular example only becomes apparent
when we consider the benefit which we gain from the dynamic length of
the BASIC strings. Imagine that we had to specify in advance the
precise length of the string so that the computer could allocate the
correct amount of memory to it in advance. We might decide to allocate,
say, 15 characters to the first name and 15 to the second name. We
would then be faced with the problem of filling up any unused space
within the storage location with spaces or some other filler. The problem
then arises if we wanted to print out the names within a sentence, that
the spaces would almost certainly be printed out too.

You will be able to observe that this problem of dealing with names
of different length arises for companies which send circulars out with
personalised inserts. If you examine these letters, you will often find that
a lot of space follows your name, particularly if it is a short one. More

sophisticated programs avoid leaving this space immediately after your name but move it instead to the end of the line.

Exercise 2.12 Extend the program which you wrote in exercise 2.9 to take the list of 25 names and print, first, a list of 25 surnames and second, a list of 25 forenames.

Example 4

Some users find BASIC very powerful because of its array-handling facilities. Mathematicians and others who need to perform matrix additions, subtractions, multiplications and inversions may be attracted by the knowledge that these operations form part of some BASICs. The program in figure 2.13 shows how simply a matrix may be entered and inverted using these facilities.

Unfortunately, most users of the language will find the matrix operations are either not implemented or are implemented only in a very restricted form. This is because matrix arithmetic takes both a lot of memory and a lot of processing power. The implementors of BASIC on microcomputers would often be faced with the option of providing only very slow matrix operations on small matrices, and choose instead not to implement them. As a result, BASIC users tend not to expect to find matrix operations and, apart from some of the larger mainframe implementations, matrix operations are rarely implemented.

```
10 REM PROGRAM 2.13
20 REM PROGRAM TO READ IN A MATRIX AND INVERT IT
30 DIM A(3,3), B(3,3)
40 MAT READ A
50 MAT B = INV(A)
60 MAT PRINT B
70 DATA 1,2,3
80 DATA 4,5,6
90 DATA 3,2,1
```

Figure 2.13

Example 5

In this example, we may see how simply a particular implementation of BASIC allows the use of simple graphics. The program listed in figure 2.14 uses RM BASIC to draw the simple boat illustrated in figure 2.15. Take careful note of the very simple BASIC commands which are used here. Unfortunately, these commands are completely implementation dependent, and changing to an alternative version would mean a complete rewrite. There is also no guarantee that corresponding commands would be available.

```
10 REM BOAT DRAWING PROGRAM

20 CLS

30 REM DRAW HULL

40 AREA 200,75;350,75;400,100;175,100

50 REM DRAW MAST

60 AREA 280,100;285,100;285,200;280,200

70 REM LEFT SAIL

80 AREA 200,110;275,110;275,200

90 REM RIGHT SAIL

100 AREA 290,110;365,110;290,200
```

Figure 2.14

For example, RM BASIC, a version of BASIC provided by the British computer manufacturer *Research Machines*, offers the CIRCLE command which allows for the drawing of a circle when the centre and

Figure 2.15

radius are specified. Another popular microcomputer implementation of the language- BBC BASIC offers no direct facility for drawing a circle, and instead a complicated method using small triangles must be used to approximate the circle.

Microsoft GW BASIC offers a very useful command BLOAD which allows for a screen display to be loaded from disk. This is particularly useful, because some of the sophisticated drawing programs provide an option to save in BSAVEd form ready to BLOAD from within a program. This can be very useful in a graphics based application.

Example 6

As a final example, figure 2.16 lists a program written in BBC BASIC which employs the BBC BASIC-specific command EVAL. EVAL allows for a mathematical function which has been inputted as a string to be evaluated at different points. It becomes easy to write programs which allow for a function to inputted interactively and plotted or (as in the present example) to produce a table of values. This facility is very powerful and useful, and could not be implemented in a compiled language since the mathematical routines to evaluate the function inputted could not be known until run-time.

```
10 REM TABLE OF VALUES
20 CLS
30 PRINT "Type in the function, using X as argument"
40 INPUT F$
50 CLS
60 PRINT "TABLE OF VALUES FOR Y=";F$
70 FOR X = 0 TO 100
80    Y = EVAL(F$)
90    PRINT X;" ";Y
100 NEXT X
```

Figure 2.16

BASIC's Limitations

As we have already identified, the main limitations of the BASIC language stem from its early introduction, its general purpose nature, and its interpretive implementation.

1) Early introduction

BASIC offers the programmer, through the provision of the GOTO statement, the opportunity to transfer execution of a program to any numbered statement within the program at any time. This has led, in some cases, to uncontrolled programmers producing 'spaghetti programs'. A spaghetti program is one where the execution of the program follows no clear pattern, but involves branching from one point to another so much that any attempt to plot the path taken would resemble a plate of spaghetti.

Modern versions of the language have sought to overcome this bad reputation which the language has earned by providing procedures and function definitions, and more sophisticated looping constructions, such as REPEAT...UNTIL or WHILE loops. The programs listed in figures 2.17 and 2.18 illustrate the use of these more structured techniques, using two alternative modern versions of the language. As usual, it is unfortunately true that the use of these newer facilities involves a departure from standard and portable code. A more portable but less well structured version is given as figure 2.19, which requires the repeated use of the GOTO statement.

```
10 REM PROGRAM 2.17

20 REM PROGRAM TO PRODUCE A MENU-DRIVEN APPLICATION

30 REPEAT

40     MENU

50     PRINT "another turn?"

60     INPUT A$

70 UNTIL (A$ = ''N")


80 PROCEDURE MENU

90 CLS

100 PRINT "SELECT REQUIRED SHAPE"
```

```
110 PRINT "1. SQUARE "

120 PRINT "2. TRIANGLE"

130 PRINT "3. RECTANGLE"

140 REPEAT

150    INPUT R

160 UNTIL (R=1) OR (R=2) OR (R=3)

170 IF R=1 THEN SQUARE ELSE IF R=2 THEN TRIANGLE ELSE
RECTANGLE

180 ENDPROC


190 PROCEDURE SQUARE

200 AREA 100,100;200,100;200,200;100,200

210 ENDPROC


220 PROCEDURE TRIANGLE

230 AREA 100,100;200,100;200,200

240 ENDPROC


250 PROCEDURE RECTANGLE

260 AREA 100,100;550,100;550,150;100,150

270 ENDPROC
```

Figure 2.17 A graphics menu-driven program using REPEAT...UNTIL and procedures in RM BASIC

```
10 REM PROGRAM 2.18

20 REM PROGRAM TO PRODUCE A MENU-DRIVEN APPLICATION

30 SCREEN 2

40 A$="Y"

50 WHILE A$ <> "N"
```

```
60      CALL MENU

70      PRINT "another turn?"

80      INPUT A$

90 WEND


100 SUB MENU

110 CLS

120 PRINT "SELECT REQUIRED SHAPE"

130 PRINT "1. SQUARE "

140 PRINT "2. TRIANGLE"

150 PRINT "3. RECTANGLE"

160 R = 6

170 WHILE (R<>1) AND (R<>2) AND (R<>3)

180     INPUT R

190 WEND

200 IF R=1 THEN CALL SQUARE ELSE IF R=2 THEN CALL
TRIANGLE ELSE CALL RECTANGLE

210 END SUB


220 SUB SQUARE

230 LINE (100,100)-(200,100)

240 LINE -(200,200)

250 LINE -(100,200)

260 LINE -(100,100)

270 END SUB


280 SUB TRIANGLE

290 LINE (100,100)-(200,100)

300 LINE -(200,200)
```

```
310 LINE -(100,100)

320 END SUB


330 SUB RECTANGLE

340 LINE (100,100)-(550,100)

350 LINE -(550,150)

360 LINE -(100,150)

370 LINE -(100,100)

380 END SUB
```

Figure 2.18 A program written in Turbo BASIC which uses WHILE loops to reproduce the action of the program in figure 2.17.

```
10 REM PROGRAM 2.19

20 REM PROGRAM TO PRODUCE A MENU-DRIVEN APPLICATION

30 REM START LOOPING

40 GOTO 90

50 PRINT "another turn?"

60 INPUT A$

70 IF A$ <> "N" THEN GOTO 30

80 END


90 REM MENU

100 CLS

110 PRINT "SELECT REQUIRED SHAPE"

120 PRINT "1. SQUARE "

130 PRINT "2. TRIANGLE"

140 PRINT "3. RECTANGLE"

150 REM START LOOPING

160 INPUT R
```

```
170 IF (R<>1) AND (R<>2) AND (R<>3) THEN GOTO 150
180 IF R=1 THEN GOTO 220
190 IF R=2 THEN GOTO 280
200 IF R=3 THEN GOTO 330
210 GOTO 50


220 REM SQUARE
230 LINE (100,100)-(200,100)
240 LINE -(200,200)
250 LINE -(100,200)
260 LINE -(100,100)
270 GOTO 210


280 REM TRIANGLE
290 LINE (100,100)-(200,100)
300 LINE -(200,200)
310 LINE -(100,100)
320 GOTO 210


330 REM RECTANGLE
340 LINE (100,100)-(550,100)
350 LINE -(550,150)
360 LINE -(100,150)
370 LINE -(100,100)
380 GOTO 210
```

Figure 2.19 This program illustrates how the same result may be obtained without using the procedures, repeat and while loops of the previous examples.

2) General purpose

General purpose languages in general suffer from the complaint that they are less well suited to each specific application than would be a special purpose language. The coding of data processing applications in BASIC is inevitably more difficult than in a business oriented language such as COBOL, and both the programmer and the subsequent user suffer from this. On the other hand, the programmer who desires the flexibility to program diverse applications using a single programming language must inevitably choose a general purpose language. BASIC then becomes an option, but where execution speed is an issue in the programs written, other, more appropriate, general purpose languages may exist.

3) Interpretive implementation

When a language is implemented using an interpreter, the execution speed of programs, particularly those involving large scale repetition of code in loops, suffers. This is because code must be translated each time it is executed, and the repeated translation of the same code within a loop is clearly very wasteful.

Just how the execution speed may be affected is illustrated very clearly in the following example. Borland's Turbo BASIC offers a compiled BASIC which is compatible with several interpreted versions based on the same hardware configuration. Figure 2.20 lists a program written to illustrate how execution speed may be affected. The final line of output gives two times: the starting and finishing times of the loop, as measured by the system's internal clock. The table in figure 2.21 shows the relative execution speeds for an interpreted version and a compiled version.

```
10 REM PROGRAM 2.20
20 T1$=TIME$
30 FOR I = 1 TO 1000
40 PRINT I, I*I, I*I*I
50 NEXT I
60 PRINT T1$,TIME$
```

Figure 2.20

Compiled Version	Interpreted Version
10 secs	21 secs

Figure 2.21

3 Pascal

Introduction

In this chapter, we meet the programming language Pascal, another language which is commonly taught in courses on programming. For reasons which will become apparent later in this chapter, Pascal is usually preferred to BASIC as the introductory language for specialist Computer Science students.

Background

Pascal is a much more recent language than BASIC, and, unlike BASIC, it has not evolved from a language designed in the early days of programming languages. Pascal was invented by Professor Niklaus Wirth of Zurich over a period of years up to 1970. A clear statement of the features of Pascal appeared in Jenson and Wirth (1975). The 1975 report acted as a definitive reference work for the language until it was superseded by an International Standards Organisation specification in 1981.

One of the major criticisms of BASIC which we formulated in chapter 2 was its non-standard nature. Programs written in BASIC for use on one particular system often have to be completely rewritten for another make of computer or in order to use the BASIC provided by a different software company. This is a problem which has been largely avoided in the provision of Pascal compilers. Pascal programs are therefore much more 'portable' than their BASIC counterparts, which is one justification for the widespread use of Pascal as a teaching language.

A second, and more fundamental, reason for the adoption of Pascal as a teaching language is that one of Wirth's design aims in establishing the language was to provide a medium through which students would learn good programming practices which could then be applied when they came to write programs in other languages.

So Pascal is respected as a 'good' language. What are the features of the language which gain favour with computer scientists?

1) Pascal is a structured language. Good programs are, by definition, well structured programs. Therefore, if a language is to be accepted as a good language, the facilities which it provides need to encourage the writing of structured programs. Pascal is able to do this through a number of features:

a) In Pascal, it is possible to group a series of language instructions (statements) together between a begin and an end and then to treat this as a single statement in a program. This helps to make a program readable as in figure 3.1. It also avoids the temptation to write the types of badly-structured programs which earlier languages such as BASIC invite because of their lack of facilities to perform several operations together without resorting to the use of branching.

b) Pascal programs may be made very readable, by careful selection of variable names (and the use of functions/procedures - see below). This helps the programmer to retain firm control over the program both

```
program fig3point1(input,output);
var
  firstno, secondno, sum : integer;
  ch : char;
begin
writeln ('Do you want to add up two numbers? (y/n)');
readln(ch);
if ch in ['y','Y'] then
  begin
```

```
    writeln('Type in first number');
    readln(firstno);
    writeln('Type in second number');
    readln(secondno);
    sum := firstno + secondno;
    writeln('The total of those two numbers is ',sum)
    end
else writeln('All right.');
writeln('End of program')
end.
```

Figure 3.1

during the initial development phase and during future debugging.

c) Well-structured programs are encouraged by the provision of very versatile procedure and function facilities. These may be used to allow reference by a name to a collection of statements which perform a clearly defined purpose, and therefore to enhance readability further. Or we may decide to set aside as a procedure a group of instructions which will be used within a program in several different places. Alternatively, when a collection of statements bracketed together by begin...end becomes so long as to make the overall program unreadable, it becomes

```
program fig3point2(input,output);
var
    firstno,secondno,sum : integer;
    ch : char;
procedure dothesum;
begin
writeln('Type in first number');
readln(firstno);
writeln('Type in second number');
```

```
readln(secondno);
sum := firstno + secondno;
writeln('The total of those two numbers is ',sum)
end;
begin
writeln ('Do you want to add up two numbers? (y/n)');
readln(ch);
if ch in ['y','Y'] then dothesum
else writeln('All right.');
writeln('End of program')
end.
```

Figure 3.2

desirable to remove those statements into a separate procedure to
enhance readability. (Figure 3.2)

d) Pascal provides a wide range of control structures for looping and
decision making. Thus we have count-controlled *for* loops and condition-
controlled loops of both *repeat/until* (exit checking) and *while/do* (entry

```
program fig3point3(input,output);
var
x,y : integer;
begin
repeat
  writeln('Type in a whole number between 1 and 5');
readln(x);
until x in [1,2,3,4,5];
case x of
  1: writeln('That is the only positive number whose
square is itself');
```

```
    2: writeln('That is the smallest even positive
number');
    3: writeln('Goldilocks met that many bears');
    4: writeln('Thats how many sides a square has');
    5:   begin
        writeln ('Here are five stars');
        for y:= 1 to x do
            write('*');
        writeln
        end
   end
   end.
```

Figure 3.3

checking) types. *If/then/else* constructions appear alongside a case statement which is more appropriate for multiple decision making (figure 3.3)

e) Pascal is a block structured language. This places Pascal in the
family of languages which developed from the language Algol 60. Block
structuring refers to the ability to define a program as consisting of a
number of blocks (where each function or procedure defines a separate
block - figure 3.4). Variables, functions and procedures (among other
things) may be declared within a particular block and are then local to
their block. In practice, this means that space is only allocated to them
on entry to the block in which they are declared, and the space is then
retrieved for use for other purposes when the program leaves their block.
The provision of block structure makes the modular development of
programs by a team feasible, and also makes it easier to develop
procedures within one program which may later be used, without modification, within other programs.

2) Pascal is a strongly-typed language, which means that every
variable used within a program must be declared before it is used. By
declaration, we mean that the programmer must list the variable by name
in an appropriate place and give details of what type of content it will

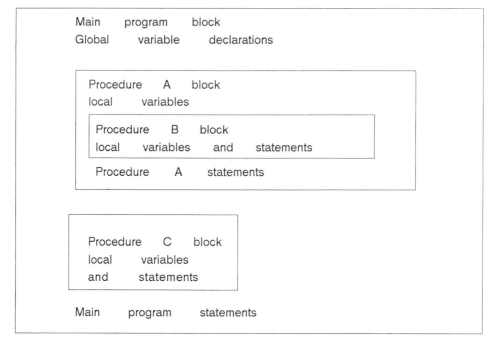

Figure 3.4 This program has 4 blocks. Procedure B is contained within the Procedure A block, which, together with the Procedure C block, lies within the outer main program block.

have. Thus, a variable called x might be declared to have the type integer, in which case only whole number values must be assigned to it. Pascal is not tolerant of mismatches between types, and will not allow values of one type to be assigned to a variable of a different type. Beginners at programming sometimes find the strong typing inconvenient, because it is easy to forget to declare a variable or to attempt an illegal assignment statement (see figures 3.5) but with more-advanced programs it often becomes apparent that the careful error checking provided by Pascal shows up typographical errors which could easily go unnoticed with the more rudimentary error checking of languages such as BASIC.

3) Pascal is a small language. Some computer languages have built into them a very large number of standard instructions, functions and procedures. Therefore in order to become proficient in programming in these languages it is necessary to learn many commands. Pascal is small

```
program fig3point5(input,output);
var
   fred,x,y,z : integer;
begin
writeln('Type in two integers');
readln(a,b); {NB a and b are not declared}
x:=2;
y:=3;
z:=y/x; {NB y/x will not be an integer so this is not
allowed}
writeln('Type in another whole number');
readln(fresd); {NB The variable name fresd is a typing
error which will be detected since no variable fresd has
been declared}
end.
```

Figure 3.5 Some examples of Pascal's error checking

in comparison, and it is possible to learn all the facilities of the language relatively quickly. It is reasonable to view this as rather a mixed blessing because one might expect the facilities on offer to be more restricted because of the smaller number of instructions available. However, there is little need to worry, because Pascal is a language which is designed to give the programmer the greatest possible opportunity to define new functions and procedures and new types of data structure which may then be used alongside the pre-defined ones. It is in fact even possible to redefine the procedures and functions supplied as part of the language if the programmer wishes to do this. Pascal is therefore very versatile in spite of its small size. Naturally, opinions vary over whether Pascal contains all the facilities desirable for a language, and we shall identify later in this chapter some of the features which would be very useful but which are not provided in standard Pascal.

4) Pascal is easy to implement and therefore widely available. When

Wirth defined the original Pascal language description, he gave thought to the requirement to design a language which could be implemented easily on computer systems. This is unusual. The designers of most languages do not consider the requirement to make them easily and efficiently implemented and therefore their languages suffer from being either available for only a small range of computers, or being more widely available in non-standard implementations because of the difficulty of producing compilers which behave as the language has been specified. To be technical, Pascal has been designed to enable 'single-pass compilation', and this, together with its small size, allows for Pascal compilers to be small and to generate efficient object code quickly. Larger languages than Pascal would have been impossible to implement on the (relatively) small memoried microcomputers of even comparatively recent years.

Who uses Pascal?

We have identified already the widespread acceptance which Pascal has received from the academic community as a teaching language. But Pascal's applications do not end with education. For the reasons described above, Pascal is standard and widely available. In particular it became one of the earliest realistic alternatives to BASIC for programming on most microcomputers.

1) Pascal offers great attractions to microcomputer software producers when compared with BASIC- which was frequently the only alternative available. Pascal is a compiled language which means that software written for sale commercially can be distributed in compiled form (i.e. without distributing the source code) and this has the attraction of making programs more difficult to reproduce with slight modification. In addition, compilation offers speed advantages when the programs are run. Until recently, the only realistic alternative for high-speed of execution on offer on many microcomputers, was assembly language, and the speed of program development in Pascal is much greater. (With the appearance of more powerful microcomputers, and therefore the implementation on microcomputers of a much wider range of high level languages, this argument is no longer quite so compelling.)

2) The standard nature of Pascal implementation saves on software development costs. Of course, this is not only true of Pascal, but is equally true of any other language where implementations stick closely to

an agreed standard. However, of the alternatives in use for developing software, Pascal is the one where standards have been adhered to more rigidly than elsewhere. This is partly because it is easy to implement, of course, but is also due to the work of the ISO in checking language compilers for Pascal and issuing certificates of compliance with the official standard. This improves the confidence of purchasers that the standard is meaningful, and motivates compiler suppliers to adhere to the standard in the knowledge that compliance is recognised.

3) In the IBM PC environment, one particular Pascal compiler- Turbo Pascal produced by Borland International, has become pre-eminent. It has been the chosen medium for the development of a substantial number of PC applications, and has enhanced still further the position of Pascal as a preferred medium for software development. Turbo Pascal was accepted by the market because it was a good, well designed product, and was offered at a very attractive price. Compared with alternative high-level language compilers on offer at the time of its original launch, Turbo Pascal was offered at 1/4 to 1/10 of the price.

This has had the effect of concentrating a lot of software development for the IBM PC and compatible machines on Borland's compiler, which has clouded the compatibility issue for Pascal. Although Turbo Pascal is not very far from the official ISO standard specification, it does not comply with that specification in a number of significant areas. To a certain extent, the changes have been introduced in the form of extensions to the standard Pascal specification to take account of several of the criticisms which we discuss later in this chapter, but these are not the only changes which Borland have introduced. Handling files, for example, is rather different in Turbo Pascal from the standard which is specified. (Figures 3.6). Borland's advertising refers to Turbo Pascal as the 'de facto standard Pascal' for the PC environment, which is clearly what it has become. Other Turbo Pascal implementations have appeared on the scene (for Apple Macintosh and CP/M 8-bit computers) and these provide compatible environments for programs with the PC Turbo compilers.

(Note: since this book is designed to allow all the programs discussed in the detailed examples to be run on micro-computers, the example programs given in this chapter have all been tested and will run satisfactorily on a Turbo Pascal system.)

```
program standardfile(input,output,datafile);
type
  name = packed array[1..20] of char;
  entry = record
       studentname:name;
       mark:integer
  end;
var
  student : entry;
  datafile : file of entry;
procedure readin(var x:name);
{a procedure to read in a name from the keyboard-
       omitted for clarity}

begin
  rewrite(datafile);
  repeat
       writeln('Type in student's name');
       readin(student.studentname);
       writeln('Type in mark');
       readln(student.mark);
       write(datafile,student)
  until student.studentname = 'End '
end.
```

Figure 3.6 a Standard Pascal to create a file of records

```
program standardfile(input,output);
type
  name = packed array[1..20] of char;
  entry = record
        studentname:name;
        mark:integer
  end;
var
  student : entry;
  datafile : file of entry;
begin
assign(datafile,'diskfilename');
rewrite(datafile);
repeat
  writeln('Type in student's name');
  readln(student.studentname);
  writeln('Type in mark');
  readln(student.mark);
  write(datafile,student)
until student.studentname = 'End ';
close(datafile)
end.
```

Figure 3.6 b Turbo Pascal to create a file of records

Pascal Applications

In this section, we shall. meet four specific examples of programs written in Pascal which perform fairly interesting tasks and illustrate some of the language facilities which are particularly characteristic of Pascal.

Example 1

The first example shows a program which is designed to accept details of the total sales receipts of each of five supermarket checkout operators every day in a particular week. This example will involve us in storing some data in the form of a table as in figure 3.7.

	Monday	Tuesday	Wednesday	Thursday	Friday	Saturday
A Smith 1						
B White 2						
C Black 3						
D Green 4						
E Jones 5						

Figure 3.7

In a language such as BASIC, we could achieve this by setting up a two-dimensional array, but we would have to refer to the days of the

```
program fig3point8a(input,output);
type
   daysofopening =
(Monday,Tuesday,Wednesday,Thursday,Friday,Saturday);
   var
      takings : array[1..5,daysofopening] of integer;
      assistant : integer; today : daysofopening;
   begin
   for today := Monday to Saturday do
      for assistant :=1 to 5 do
            begin
            case today of
                  Monday : writeln('Monday');
                  Tuesday : writeln('Tuesday');
                  Wednesday : writeln('Wednesday');
                  Thursday : writeln('Thursday');
                  Friday : writeln('Friday');
                  Saturday : writeln('Saturday')
            end;
            writeln('Assistant number ',assistant,' enter
takings');
            readln(takings[assistant,today])
            end;
      writeln('End of data entry')
   end.
```

Figure 3.8a Program to illustrate entry of a table indexed by days of the week.

week by number rather than any more convenient representation, and the program would therefore be rather less readable than the example listed in figure 3.8a.

Notice the use of the TYPE declaration in order to set up the enumerated type 'daysofweek' which is then used in both the array declaration for the sales receipts and also for the control variable of the FOR loop. It is unfortunate that the value of the enumerated type cannot be used in a WRITELN statement since then it would be much more easy to produce the user-friendly program without the use of the CASE statement required here.

Exercise 3.8b Try to rewrite the program given so that it uses a second enumerated type 'assistants' to refer to the checkout operators by name instead of by number (as in figure 3.7).

Example 2

In this second example, we are going to store a list of the names, addresses and salary levels of 50 employees of a company in a table. We also wish to store this table on disk. The entry in the table which corresponds to a particular employee is illustrated in figure 3.9, and a program which accomplishes this is shown as figure 3.10.

Surname	Smith
Forename	Frederick
Address 1	10 High Street
Address 2	Anyplace
Address 3	Thiscounty
Address 4	POST CODE
Salary	21713

Figure 3.9

```pascal
program fig3point10(input,output,datafile);
type
   string20 = packed array [1..20] of char;
   employee = record
        surname:string20;
        forename:string20;
        add1:string20;
        add2:string20;
        add3:string20;
        add4:string20;
        salary:integer
   end;
var
   current:employee;
   count:integer;
   datafile:file of employee;
   table : array [1..50] of employee;
procedure readinstring(var x:string20);
var
   count,k:integer;
begin
count:=1;
while (not eoln) and (count <= 20) do
 begin
  read(x[count]);
  count:=count+1
end;
readln;
```

```
for k:=count to 20 do
  x[k]:=' ';
 end;
procedure todisk;
 var
  count : integer;
begin
rewrite(datafile);
for count :=1 to 50 do
begin
  datafile^:=table[count];
  put(datafile)
end
end;

begin
for count := 1 to 50 do
 begin
  writeln('Employee number ',count);
  write('Type in surname ');
  readinstring(current.surname);
  write('Forename ');
  readinstring(current.forename);
  write('Address line 1 ');
  readinstring(current.add1);
  write(' 2 ');
  readinstring(current.add2);
  write(' 3 ');
  readinstring(current.add3);
```

```
write (' 4 ');
readinstring(current.add4);
write ('Salary ');
readln(current.salary);
table[count]:=current
end;
writeln('To disk');
todisk
end.
```

Figure 3.10

In figure 3.9, it is clear that we need to store a collection of information about each employee (an employee record) which subdivides naturally into a series of distinct subsections (fields). Some of the fields need to contain string data (i.e. a mixture of numerical and alphabetic) while the salary column would most conveniently be stored as a whole number (integer). In Pascal, we may do this by using a record construction to define the shape of each employee record and then set up an array (or list) of these employee records. In other words, the Pascal language, via the TYPE statement, is allowing us to set up a data structure which exactly matches up with the true underlying structure of the data.

We may observe here, however, the inconvenience of dealing with strings of alphanumeric data in Pascal. We shall return to this theme in the next section.

Also within the example program, you will observe the use of several procedures where pieces of code which together perform a discernible task are grouped. Some of the parameters listed in brackets after the procedure's name are preceded by the word *var* and variables whose names are passed as variable parameters may have their values changed by the procedure (as in this case, where the variable whose name is passed to the procedure will assume the value typed in at the keyboard).

Parameters which are listed without the word var are value parameters and variables whose names are passed as value parameters will maintain their previous values on exit from the procedure.

The procedure which puts the data to file is called 'Todisk' and illustrates how a file may be set up on disk which can contain records of a predetermined 'shape'. These records are then written to the file one-by-one by the procedure. Note that figure 3.11 lists an alternative form of the procedure 'Todisk' for use with Turbo Pascal.

Note: If you are not using Turbo Pascal it is likely that you will need to refer to your Pascal system user guide to determine how to set up a disk file to contain your data.

Corresponding to the program in figure 3.10, figure 3.12 lists a program which may be used to retrieve the contents of the file created above. The new program prints a list of the names of all workers with a salary level in excess of twenty thousand pounds. Naturally, you will have to run the earlier program to create the file before running the new program to find out its contents!

```
procedure todisk;
var
  count : integer;
begin
assign(datafile,'a:datafile.tmp');
rewrite(datafile);
for count :=1 to 2 do
  write(datafile,table[count])
end;
```

Figure 3.11 Turbo Pascal version of procedure 'Todisk'

```pascal
program fig3point12(input,output,datafile);
type
string20 = packed array [1..20] of char;
 employee = record
   surname:string20;
   forename:string20;
   add1:string20;
   add2:string20;
   add3:string20;
   add4:string20;
   salary:integer
end;
var
current:employee;
count:integer;
datafile:file of employee;
table : array[1..50] of employee;
procedure fromdisk;
var
   count : integer;
begin
reset(datafile);
for count :=1 to 50 do
   read(datafile,table[count])
end;
```

```
begin
fromdisk;
for count := 1 to 50 do
  begin
  current:=table[count];
  writeln('Employee number ',count);
  write('Surname ');
  writeln(current.surname);
  write('Forename ');
  writeln(current.forename);
  write('Address line 1 ');
  writeln(current.add1);
  write(' 2 ');
  writeln(current.add2);
  write(' 3 ');
  writeln(current.add3);
  write(' 4 ');
  writeln(current.add4);
  write('Salary ');
  writeln(current.salary);
  end
end.
```

Figure 3.12

Exercise 3.13 By referring to the programs above, create a file
containing the names and two favourite subjects of each of a class of
fifteen students. Write a second program which prints out a list of all
those students who selected 'French' as their first choice subject.

Example 3

The program listed in figure 3.14 illustrates a very powerful technique, known as recursion. Pascal (along with most other modern
languages) allows a procedure or function to be defined in terms of
itself or 'recursively' as in the case of the factorial function listed here.

The factorial function is useful in a variety of mathematical applications, and is defined for any positive integer to be the product of all the
whole numbers from one up to the number given: thus factorial(2)=1*2=2
factorial(5)=1*2*3*4*5=120 and so on. Clearly, for x greater than one,
factorial(x) = factorial(x - 1) * x which leads to the recursive definition
given.

```
program fig3point14(input,output);
var
  number:integer;
  function factorial(x:integer) :integer;
begin
if x = 0 then factorial:=1
  else factorial := x * factorial(x-1)
end;


begin
writeln('Type in a positive integer');
{N.B. because of limitations on the size of the answer,
some computers will not give the correct answer for numbers
larger than about 7!}
readln(number);
writeln('The factorial of ',number,' is
',factorial(number))
end.
```

Figure 3.14

Exercise 3.15 You will not be able to use an unlimited number of levels of recursion (i.e. a procedure which is allowed to call itself an excessively large number of times will result in an error becoming apparent). Experiment to find out what sort of limit this is for your computer system and see what happens when the limit is exceeded.

Example 4

The final example program (given in figure 3.16) gives an implementation of a classical game 'Animals'. The computer gradually sets up a decision tree similar to figure 3.17 on the basis of a series of users teaching it about characteristics of new animals. This is an early example of the computer learning from its experience and showing rudimentary 'intelligence'.

```
program animals(input,output);
type
   string40 = packed array [1..40] of char;
   pointer = ^node;
   node = record
          content : string40;
          left : pointer;
          right : pointer
      end;
var
   head,current,oldnode,previous,next : pointer;
   ch : char;
   finished : boolean;

procedure readinstring(var x:string40);
var
   count,k:integer;
begin
count:=1;
```

```
while (not eoln) and (count <= 40) do
  begin
  read(x[count]);
  count:=count+1
  end;
readln;
for k:=count to 40 do
  x[k]:=' ';
end;


procedure addanimal;
begin
new(oldnode);
oldnode^ := current^;
new(next);
next^.left := nil;
next^.right := nil;
writeln('I do not know your animal. Please type in its
name.');
  readinstring(next^.content);
writeln('What yes/no question should I ask to
distinguish between a ',current^.content, ' and a
',next^.content,'?');
  readinstring(current^.content);
writeln('what would be the answer for a
',next^.content);
  readln(ch);
if (ch = 'y') or (ch = 'Y') then
  begin
  current^.left := next;
```

```
            current^.right := oldnode
            end
        else
            begin
            current^.left := oldnode;
             current^.right := next
            end
        end;
        begin
        new(head);
        head^.content :='Elephant ';
        head^.left := nil;
        head^.right := nil;
        repeat
            finished:=false;
            writeln('Think of an animal. The computer will try to
guess what it is.');
            current := head;
                repeat
                if current^.left = nil then
                    begin
                    finished := true;
                    writeln('Is it a ',current^.content,'?');
                    readln(ch);
                    if (ch = 'n') or (ch = 'N') then addanimal else
writeln ('O.K.')
                    end
                else
                    begin
```

```
writeln(current^.content);
readln(ch);
if (ch = 'y') or (ch = 'Y') then
     begin
     previous := current;
     current := current^.left
     end
else
     begin
     previous := current;
     current := current^.right
     end
end
until (previous^.left = nil) or finished;
writeln('Another go?');
readln(ch)
until (ch = 'n') or (ch = 'N')
end.
```

Figure 3.16

The animals program illustrates the use of dynamic data structures in Pascal. The tree is not set up initially to have a particular predefined shape, but instead, additional branches are added as required in the necessary places (figure 3.18). This is often a useful strategy to adopt in situations where we cannot predict in advance, with any degree of certainty, how much data is required in a particular place within a data structure. Linked lists and tree structures are commonly implemented using these dynamic data handling techniques- characterised by the use of pointer variables and the procedure new. This illustrates once again the flexibility available to the Pascal programmer despite the rigorous requirements to declare all the static variables to be used within the program.

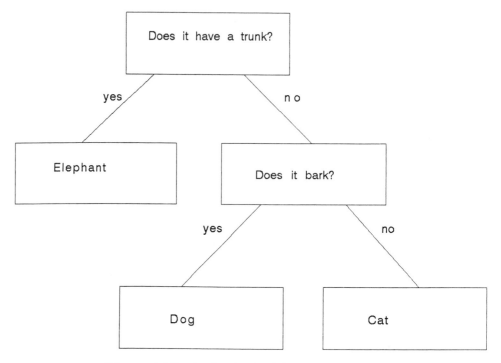

Figure 3.17 A simple decision tree

Exercise 3.19 The program animals listed in figure 3.16 knows only the animal 'elephant' Try running the program and teaching the computer about new animals. (Unfortunately, when you stop playing the game, the computer will forget all its new found knowledge!)

Pascal's limitations

As we have already identified, Pascal is a flexible language which can be adapted to do almost anything which we are likely to need. Therefore its limitations are mainly those areas where it seems unnecessarily complicated.

1) Very simple programs: Pascal is a language which has a rigid set of rules. These rules must be followed rigorously, and therefore the

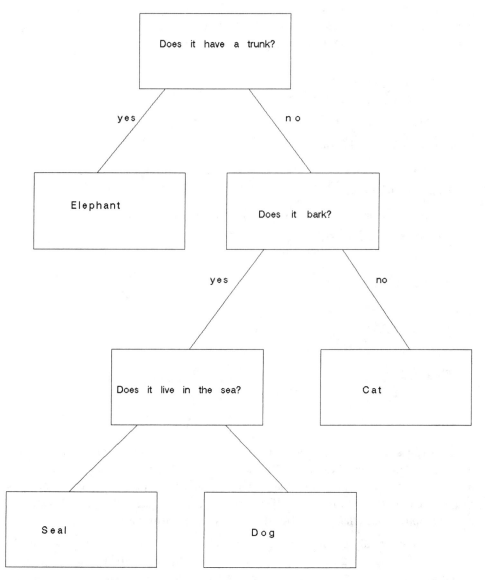

Figure 3.18 Here the decision tree from 3.17 is developed to add an extra animal

extremely simple two or three line BASIC program becomes a seven or eight line Pascal program. (Figure 3.20).

This can seem unnecessarily complicated to the beginner. On the other hand, Pascal's flexibility means that almost any longer program will be substantially shorter in Pascal than in BASIC.

BASIC Program

```
10 REM Simple addition
20 INPUT "Type in two numbers"; A,B
30 PRINT "The sum is ";A+B
```

Pascal equivalent

```
program simpleaddition(input,output);
var a,b : integer;
begin
writeln('Type in two numbers');
readln(a,b);
writeln('The sum is ',a+b)
end.
```

Figure 3.20

2) Programs which require direct access to the computer hardware or assembly language: Standard Pascal does not provide any access to assembly language and machine code routines. Some implementations provide extensions which do offer this, but as a general rule, Pascal is not the appropriate language for these low-level programs.

3) String handling: Surprisingly, Pascal does not support any standard methods for inputting a string of characters. Instead, strings have to be accepted as a series of characters, each read in separately. This is tedious in the extreme (see figure 3.21) and has resulted in almost all modern implementations incorporating extensions to the language which

offer facilities to read in strings in a single instruction.

The reason for Pascal's lack of a string input procedure is largely historical. In 1975, interactive programs were not nearly as common as they are today, and therefore the input to a Pascal program was typically from a file of characters already stored within the computer system somewhere. The entire file therefore consisted of a series of characters, interspersed with end of line markers to distinguish the different lines of the file (figures 3.22). Character handling routines were required regularly to take in the values from the input file, and therefore routines to handle string input were developed alongside the other input routines within each application. It is the arrival of interactive programming with the personal computer which has made the omission of simple string input routines a major difficulty.

```
procedure readinstring(var x:string20);
{This procedure reads in a string of up to 20 characters}
var
   count,k:integer;
begin
count:=1;
while (not eoln) and (count <= 20) do
   begin
   read(x[count]);
   count:=count+1
   end;
readln;
for k:=count to 20 do x[k]:=' ';
end;
```

Figure 3.21

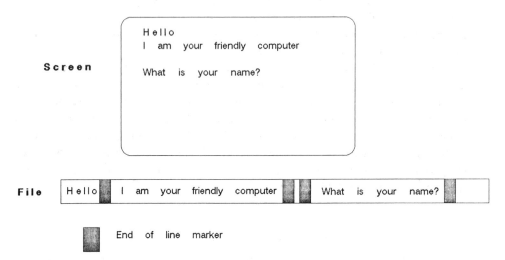

Figure 3.22 The text shown on the screen corresponds to the file listed below

4) Special purposes: Pascal was originally developed, as we discussed earlier in this chapter, from a variety of motives, but without any specific area of programming application in mind. It therefore has the feature of wide applicability (as a general purpose computer language) but lacks the special features which would make it particularly efficient in any individual application area. It is therefore a good language to know, but could almost always be bettered for a particular application by a more application-specific language.

4 COBOL

Introduction

This chapter looks at the programming language COBOL, which is one of the longest established computer programming languages still in general use. COBOL is commonly used in business data processing applications.

Background

The language COBOL- COmmon Business Oriented Language was first introduced in the USA in 1959 as a high level language suitable for use in writing programs which could handle efficiently large amounts of data in file processing applications. It was designed alongside an early generation of computer hardware, and many features of the language as it was used at that time were specifically aimed at the efficient use of the computer facilities of the day.

The responsibility for maintaining and developing the COBOL language has been undertaken by a voluntary organisation: the Conference on Data Systems Languages (CODASYL). The first COBOL standard specification (COBOL 68) was proposed by the American standards Institute in 1966. This was based upon the CODASYL recommendations current at the end of 1965 but was not finally agreed until 1968.

Today's COBOL programmers have additional features available to them, becase newer versions of the language have been introduced which allow the use of more modern computer facilities. The most usual implementations of the language in use today are therefore either based on the ANSI-74 standard specification for COBOL, or, increasingly commonly, based upon ANSI-85 COBOL. These standards were introduced, respectively, in about 1974 and in about 1985, although draft versions of the standards were available somewhat earlier.

When a computer language evolves as COBOL has, new versions of the language are inevitably a compromise. The committees who meet to specify a new version are faced with a dilemma. They want to design a new version which takes into account changes in hardware design and facilities, and new ways of thinking about problem solving. On the other hand, if a new version of a language is to provide 'upwards compatibility' with previous versions, then it is essential that programs developed in the previous version will continue to run in the new version.

This upwards compatibility is crucial to the widespread acceptance of the new version of a programming language, since the cost of purchasing upgrades for a compiler are extremely small when set against the value of the programs which are written using that compiler. The scenario where some users choose to upgrade for the extra facilities on offer while others prefer to continue to use a previous version in order to avoid reprogramming is one which must be avoided at all costs, since it makes support and the provision of developmental tools very difficult. This puts pressure on those who design a new version to avoid radical changes to the language, and accounts for the sometimes rather unnatural ways in which programs must be written using these 'older' computer languages.

Most computer applications today involve data processing. Large quantites of mainly non-numerical data are processed in various ways. For example, many companies use computers to maintain details of the names and addresses of suppliers and creditors and use the computer to write letters and to process invoices and orders. Other large scale uses of computers are for personnel and payroll activities. In each of these examples, some numerical processing of the data is going on, but it is the performance of a large number of essentially simple calculations, and contrasts with the high-powered mathematical calculations which were performed on the earliest computers, usually for military purposes.

COBOL entered the arena at the point when data processing applications were first being introduced, while other languages (notably FORTRAN) were introduced at a similar time for the use of scientists and others who needed high powered 'number crunching' facilities. It is important to remember this pioneering nature of the COBOL language when we begin to look in detail at its facilities.

A cursory glance at any COBOL program will yield some information about the language. Figure 4.1 shows a simple COBOL program, and we may observe that the program is sub-divided into a series of divisions. Each division has its own particular purpose and contains language statements which fulfil a particular purpose.

```
0001 IDENTIFICATION DIVISION.

0002    PROGRAM-ID. PROG4POINT1.

0003 ENVIRONMENT DIVISION.

0004 CONFIGURATION SECTION.

0005    SOURCE-COMPUTER. IBM PC.

0006 DATA DIVISION.

0007 WORKING-STORAGE SECTION.

0008    77 FIRST-NUMBER PIC 999.

0009    77 SECOND-NUMBER PIC 999.

0010    77 TOTAL-NUMBER PIC 9999.

0011 PROCEDURE DIVISION.

0012 BEGIN.

0013    ACCEPT FIRST-NUMBER.

0014    ACCEPT SECOND-NUMBER.

0015    ADD FIRST-NUMBER TO SECOND-NUMBER GIVING
TOTAL-NUMBER.

0016    DISPLAY TOTAL-NUMBER.

0017 STOP RUN.
```

Figure 4.1 A COBOL program which adds two numbers together and outputs their sum (Not user-friendly).

In the present example, the IDENTIFICATION DIVISION contains details about the program's name, and the ENVIRONMENT DIVISION contains information about the computer on which the program was developed. The DATA DIVISION contains descriptions of the variables which will be used, and it is normal to use the identification number 77 against simple variables of this type. We shall see later how record structures may be created by varying this number. The PROCEDURE DIVISION contains the actual statements which are executed when the program is run.

A slightly closer look at the program reveals that COBOL is a discursive language. It invites the programmer to write in a rather long-winded way. This reflects the desire of those who designed the original COBOL language to provide a computer language which was different from its competitors and which was acceptable for use in business. It was important to persuade business people that the computer's purpose and usefulness could be explained across the management, and no just to the specialist programmers. Most COBOL programs can therefore be read fairly easily, and there are few commands whose purpose is not reasonably clear. This clarity of written language is reinforced by the use of the terms 'sentence' and 'paragraph' to describe the subdivisions of a COBOL program. The use of these familiar terms helps to encourage the non-computer specialist to realise that the COBOL program resembles closely a series of instructions to the computer written in English.

The program in figure 4.1 has the sentences within the PROCEDURE DIVISION grouped into a single paragraph named 'BEGIN'. The statements within the program are numbered for convenience, the numbers do not play any significant part in the execution of the program.

The disadvantage of COBOL's discursive style is that many programmers who have developed their skills using other languages find COBOL a very inconvenient language in which to program. Figure 4.2 gives the listing of a program similar to the one given in figure 4.1, but with more user friendly features, which adds together two numbers and outputs their sum. The corresponding Pascal and BASIC programs are also given for comparison. It is a natural consequence of the long winded COBOL statements that COBOL source files should typically be longer than corresponding code in alternative languages. With very complex programs this can be inconvenient if the editor's capacity is limited.

```
0001 IDENTIFICATION DIVISION.

0002   PROGRAM-ID. PROG4POINT2.

0003 ENVIRONMENT DIVISION.

0004 CONFIGURATION SECTION.

0005   SOURCE-COMPUTER. IBM PC.

0006 DATA DIVISION.

0007 WORKING-STORAGE SECTION.

0008   77 FIRST-NUMBER PIC 999.

0009   77 SECOND-NUMBER PIC 999.

0010   77 TOTAL-NUMBER PIC 9999.

0011 PROCEDURE DIVISION.

0012 BEGIN.

0013   DISPLAY "ENTER FIRST NUMBER ".

0014   ACCEPT FIRST-NUMBER.

0015   DISPLAY "ENTER SECOND NUMBER ".

0016   ACCEPT SECOND-NUMBER.

0017   ADD FIRST-NUMBER TO SECOND-NUMBER GIVING
TOTAL-NUMBER.

0018   DISPLAY "THEIR TOTAL IS ".

0019   DISPLAY TOTAL-NUMBER.

0020 STOP RUN.
```

Figure 4.2a COBOL program to add two numbers and output their sum. (User friendly version)

```
10 REM PROGRAM TO ADD TWO NUMBERS

20 INPUT "TYPE IN FIRST NUMBER "; N1

30 INPUT "TYPE IN SECOND NUMBER "; N2

40 SUM = N1 + N2

50 PRINT "THEIR SUM IS "; SUM
```

Figure 4.2b BASIC program corresponding to figure 4.2a.

```
program fig4point2(input,output);
var
  n1,n2,sum : integer;
begin
writeln('Type in first number ');
readln(n1);
writeln('Type in second number ');
readln(n2);
sum := n1 + n2;
writeln('Their sum is ',sum)
end.
```

Figure 4.2c Pascal equivalent of COBOL program in figure 4.2a.

A second feature of COBOL which was inevitable in the early 1960's is its use of upper case characters grouped into 80-character lines of program. Programs at that time were invariably prepared on coding sheets and then transferred to punched cards or paper tape. Punched cards allowed up to 80 characters to be inputted on a single card, and therefore the coding sheets were designed to reflect this, and the language structure followed. Early input/output facilities only offered upper case characters and therefore the language was limited by this. Modern facilities impose no such limitations, but the COBOL language has nevertheless retained these features.

Within each 80 character line of a COBOL program, the actual program instructions are contained within columns 8 to 72. Columns 1 to 6 form 2 margins: they contain the program line number, which is usually represented as a 3 digit page number followed by a three digit line number. As with BASIC lines of code, it is normal to number the lines in a sequence of multiples of 10 (10, 20, 30, 40 etc) in order to allow for the subsequent insertion of additional lines. The numbering of the pages relates to the use of coding sheets to list the lines of a COBOL program. It is convenient to have each coding sheet numbered. Column 7 provides a space for a continuity marker '-' which is used when the line above was not long enough to hold the entire COBOL sentence. The next line on the coding sheet then becomes a part of the previous line, to enable longer sentences of code to be input. The continuity marker used to be used in order to indicate to the compiler that a punched card should be linked with its predecessor during compilation. Columns 73 to 80 are ignored by the compiler, and are often used for inserting a heading or comments in the program listing. (See figure 4.3)

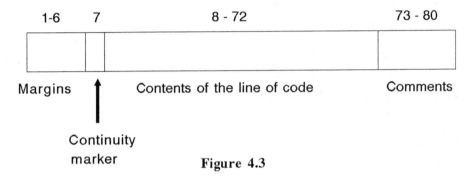

Figure 4.3

So a COBOL program is made up of a series of sentences. Each sentence ends with a full stop, and the sentences may be grouped into paragraphs. Each paragraph within a program is given a name, and we shall see later that the names of the paragraphs are very useful in controlling the execution of the program.

COBOL's facilities

Crucial to the operation of any programming language in a data processing environment are the data structures which it offers and the ways in which these data structures may be manipulated. Naturally, COBOL is very strong in this area, particularly when one considers how long ago the initial specification for the language was released. Principally, we shall be concerned with two main types of data-structure: the table, and the file.

COBOL provides facilities for setting up tables of data of any number of dimensions. These tables must be defined in the DATA DIVISION of the program in order that the appropriate storage may be allocated, and then they are used very much like arrays in other languages. The tables may be of a record structure, which means that some quite complicated mixtures of variable types are allowed. Figure 4.4a illustrates a simple 1-dimensional table which may be set up using the DATA DIVISION coding given in figure 4.4b.

Ref	Surname	Title	Initial	Age
019	Smith	Mrs	F	32
025	Jones	Miss	A	26
031	Brown	Miss	D	41
045	White	Mr	B	27

Figure 4.4a   A simple 1-dimensional table

```
DATA DIVISION.
WORKING-STORAGE SECTION.
  01 TABLE-1.
     02 PERSON-VALUE OCCURS 7 TIMES.
        03 REF-NO PIC 999.
        03 SURNAME PIC A(20).
        03 TITLE PIC A(5).
        03 INITIAL PIC A.
        03 AGE PIC 99.
```

Figure 4.4b The COBOL code to set up the storage for the simple table shown in figure 4.4a.

Looking at figure 4.4b, we may begin to understand the significance of the numbers 01, 02, 03 etc. These numbers represent the level of description. Thus, at the outermost level (01), we see TABLE-1, which is made up of 7 PERSON-VALUEs each of which is made up of a REF, a SURNAME, a TITLE, an INITIAL, and an AGE. The PIC verb allows us to describe accurately what the data will look like: PIC 99 means two digits, PIC A means 1 alphabetic character, and PIC A(20) means 20 alphabetic characters, for example.

File processing in COBOL is probably as sophisticated as in any language. Serial, sequential and random file access methods are supported, the random files generally being implemented by indexed sequential access method. Not only is it possible to create all these different types of file, but the COBOL language is very supportive of the programmer who wishes to use them. It provides, for example, the SORT verb to enable the easy translation from a serial file (which is unsorted) to a sequential file (which contains the same records, but in a sorted form). (Figure 4.5).

```
0001 IDENTIFICATION DIVISION.

0002   PROGRAM-ID. PROG4POINT5.

0003 ENVIRONMENT DIVISION.

0004 INPUT-OUTPUT SECTION.

0005 FILE-CONTROL.

0006 SELECT SEQ-FILE-TMP ASSIGN TO DISK.

0007 SELECT SEQ-FILE-UNSORTED ASSIGN TO DISK.

0008 SELECT SEQ-FILE ASSIGN TO DISK.

0009 DATA DIVISION.

0010 FILE SECTION.

0011 SD SEQ-FILE-TMP.

0012   01 RECORD-TMP.

0013       02 REF-NO-TMP PIC 99.

0014       02 SURNAME-TMP PIC A(20).

0015       02 TITLE-TMP PIC A(5).

0016       02 INITIAL-TMP PIC A.

0017       02 AGE-TMP PIC 99.

0018 FD SEQ-FILE-UNSORTED.

0019 LABEL RECORDS ARE STANDARD.

0020 VALUE OF FILE-ID IS "FILEIN".

0021   01 RECORD-1.

0022       02 REF-NO-1 PIC 99.
```

```
0023        02 SURNAME-1 PIC A(20).

0024        02 TITLE-1 PIC A(5).

0025        02 INITIAL-1 PIC A.

0026        02 AGE-1 PIC 99.

0027 FD SEQ-FILE.

0028 LABEL RECORDS ARE STANDARD.

0029 VALUE OF FILE-ID IS "FILEOUT".

0030   01 RECORD-2.

0031        02 REF-NO-2 PIC 99.

0032        02 SURNAME-2 PIC A(20).

0033        02 TITLE-2 PIC A(5).

0034        02 INITIAL-2 PIC A.

0035        02 AGE-2 PIC 99.

0036 PROCEDURE DIVISION.

0037 BEGIN.

0038    SORT SEQ-FILE-TMP ON ASCENDING KEY SURNAME-TMP
USING SEQ-FILE-UNSORTED GIVING SEQ-FILE.

0039 STOP RUN.
```

Figure 4.5 A simple program using the SORT verb to sort a serial file and give a sequential file.

The SORT verb requires the specification of three files of identical structure. The unsorted serial file is converted into a sorted sequential file by the SORT command, which must use a temporary working file defined using an SD statement, in the process. The other two files are described using FD statements. It is possible to sort the file in ascending or descending order based upon the values within any 'key' field. The form of the SORT sentence is therefore:

```
SORT <file-name-1> ON ASCENDING KEY <fieldname(s)>

USING <file-name-2>

GIVING <file-name-3>.
```

Here, file-name-1 is the working file, file-name-2 is the unsorted file, and file-name-3 is the sorted file.

COBOL is also flexible in allowing the programmer to specify the key field within the records of a file. Other complex file-handling facilties provided by COBOL include the MERGE command, which allows two compatible sequential files to be merged into a new file in the corresponding sequence, and the ability to specify alternative access methods for indexed sequential files which can be accessed sequentially, by index or dynamically. More details of these techniques appear later in this chapter.

Closely linked with the need to provide good facilities for the processing of sophisticated data-structures, is the need to provide good input/output facilities for the programmer. The larger implementations of COBOL provide a 'Report Writer' facility which enables sophisticated reports to be prepared very easily by the programmer. The report writer deals with such aspects of the task as providing headings on each page of a written report, and spacing out the output over an appropriate number of pages.

Smaller implementations of the language are unable to provide this report writer facility, which is not in any case demanded by the standard, because the provision of these sophisticated facilities takes up a lot of space, and COBOL is, by most standards, a large language. However, it is always possible for a programmer to produce the reports for himself by using the usual range of outputting facilities.

COBOL was not designed as a particularly structured language, which is hardly surprising given the timing of its introduction, but there is nevertheless the facility to control program flow in a more sophisticated way than just using the simple GO-TO verb. The use of PERFORM allows for a particular paragraph of the program to be executed just as if it were a procedure. Execution returns to the PERFORM statement at the end of the called paragraph. Several consecutive paragraphs may be executed in this way by the use of the THRU qualifier in a PERFORM command. (Figure 4.6).

```
0001 IDENTIFICATION DIVISION.

0002   PROGRAM-ID. PROG4POINT6.

0003 ENVIRONMENT DIVISION.

0004 DATA DIVISION.
```

```
0005 WORKING-STORAGE SECTION.
0006    77 NUM1 PIC 9.
0007    77 NUM2 PIC 9.
0008    77 SUM PIC 99.
0009 PROCEDURE DIVISION.
0010 PARA-1.
0011    DISPLAY "TYPE IN A NUMBER ".
0012    ACCEPT NUM1.
0013 PARA-2.
0014    DISPLAY "TYPE IN ANOTHER NUMBER ".
0015    ACCEPT NUM2.
0016 PARA-3.
0017    DISPLAY "THE TOTAL IS ".
0018    ADD NUM1 TO NUM2 GIVING SUM.
0019    DISPLAY SUM.
0020 AGAIN.
0021    PERFORM PARA-1 THRU PARA-3.
0022 STOP RUN.
```

Figure 4.6 Program illustrating the use of the PERFORM...THRU construction.

COBOL 85 provides a good level of portability across different implementations. As such, it is one of the more portable computer languages for the development of high level applications. Unfortunately, microcomputer implementations of the language often suffer from the large size of the language specification, and sometimes are therefore unable to meet the full specification.

Who uses COBOL?

The question 'Who uses COBOL?' would have been extremely easy to answer in the late 1970's because, at that time, COBOL had really no realistic competitors in the field of data-processing. The result was that, in any organisation which was concerned with large scale data processing activities, the COBOL language was the language of choice for implementing the programs. Data processing departments of most larger companies would have had a team of COBOL programmers for developing new applications and maintaining older software.

The situation today is more complex. We may best assess it by considering separately three groups of companies:

1) Those who historically have used COBOL:

These are mainly the larger companies, who entered the data processing field in the 1960's and 1970's. For these users, the existing commitment to the COBOL language is often sufficient to keep them continuing to use the same language. We identified this inbuilt inertia earlier in the chapter as being a significant restriction on the flexbility of the language to adapt to suit the newer hardware and working methods, and it is also no less an influence in retaining COBOL users in the face of competition from other languages.

But not all companies involved in data processing today are tied to the COBOL language in this way. Some of the larger companies have already moved away from the use of COBOL towards other alternatives. Some companies have moved over to C, many others have moved away from 'traditional' styles of programming languages altogether for their applications generation. Many have adopted database management languages such as DBase and SQL (Structured Query Language) and other very highly specialised packages which are especially designed to suit the needs of the modern data processing applications, and allow the development time for applications programs to be kept at a minimum.

2) More recent entrants to the Data Processing field:

Those companies which entered the computerised data processing field late, or those smaller companies which concentrate their computer uses on smaller computers have usually not used COBOL. This is partly because, as a big computer language, COBOL was often not a realistic alternative for the users of small computer systems, because it was either unavailable, or was only available in a rather restrictive version. As a result, much of the upsurge in data processing use by smaller companies comes from those who have historically used other languages.

There is therefore in this group a substantial commitment to 'inappropriate' languages for data processing such as BASIC, and also to other languages which may have been selected more because a particular employee has recommended it than because of any well thought out strategy.

3) The package purchaser:

Those who begin to use computers for data processing today often adopt the packaged solution to their problems, by purchasing a suitable piece of software ready written and tested. This avoids the necessity to have a team in a programming department who are involved in the development and maintenance of the software. Naturally these users fall outside the scope of this book, but the packages which they purchase will have been developed in a suitable high-level language. Some will have been developed in COBOL, but today, many more are developed in C and other more modern languages.

It is clear from the above discussion, that COBOL's stranglehold on the data processing market has been relaxed of late. It is still a significant language, because those users who are still tied to COBOL applications exert a steady influence on the marketplace, both in their demands for compilers and libraries and in their demands for experienced COBOL programmers. It remains the experience of the author, that more students request a knowledge of COBOL in order to enhance their employability than ask about all other major high level languages combined.

If we attempt to answer the question as to whether an organisation first setting up a data processing department should choose COBOL as the preferred language or some alternative, we are faced with a somewhat difficult question to answer. In terms of the facilities on offer to the programmer for specifically data processing applications, it is hard to come near to the COBOL facilities in any other language, although C and Modula-2 do provide a reasonable range of these facilities through commonly available add-on libraries. On the other hand, from the point of view of writing programs in a modern way, and being flexible to allow programmers to work in other areas (not data processing) within a company, it might well be considered desirable to select one of these more general purpose computer languages which can also cope with the data processing demands being made.

COBOL Applications

In this section, we will meet some realistic applications examples which employ the programming language COBOL in typical business problems.

Example 1

This first example illustrates a very simple calculation of commission for a salesman who sells items of three different classes: A, B, C. The commission payable on sales of class A is 5%, on sales of class B is 10% and on sales of class C is 20%. The program allows the user to type in a list of sales, entering in each case the class and the amount of money, and produces the value of total commission at the end of the list.

The program is listed in figure 4.7, and some samples of dialogue with the program in use are given in figure 4.8.

```
0001 IDENTIFICATION DIVISION.

0002    PROGRAM-ID. PROG4POINT7.

0003 ENVIRONMENT DIVISION.

0004 DATA DIVISION.

0005 WORKING-STORAGE SECTION.

0006    77 COMMISSION-SO-FAR PIC 999.99.

0007    77 PRODUCT-CODE PIC A.

0008    77 PRODUCT-VALUE PIC 999.99.

0009 PROCEDURE DIVISION.

0010 BEGIN.

0011    MOVE ZERO TO COMMISSION-SO-FAR.

0012 NEXT-PRODUCT.

0013    DISPLAY "TYPE IN PRODUCT CODE Z TO FINISH".

0014    ACCEPT PRODUCT-CODE.

0015    IF PRODUCT-CODE = "Z" GO TO END-OF-LIST.

0016    DISPLAY "TYPE IN VALUE OF SALES".

0017    ACCEPT PRODUCT-VALUE.
```

```
0018 TYPE-A.
0019   IF PRODUCT-CODE NOT = "A" GO TO TYPE-B.
0020   MULTIPLY 0.05 BY PRODUCT-VALUE.
0021   ADD PRODUCT-VALUE TO COMMISSION-SO-FAR.
0022   GO TO NEXT-PRODUCT.
0023 TYPE-B.
0024   IF PRODUCT-CODE NOT = "B" GO TO TYPE-C.
0025   MULTIPLY 0.1 BY PRODUCT-VALUE.
0026   ADD PRODUCT-VALUE TO COMMISSION-SO-FAR.
0027   GO TO NEXT-PRODUCT.
0028 TYPE-C.
0029   IF PRODUCT-CODE NOT = "C" GO TO NEXT-PRODUCT.
0030   MULTIPLY 0.2 BY PRODUCT-VALUE.
0031   ADD PRODUCT-VALUE TO COMMISSION-SO-FAR.
0032   GO TO NEXT-PRODUCT.
0033 END-OF-LIST.
0034   DISPLAY "TOTAL COMMISSION= "
0035   DISPLAY COMMISSION-SO-FAR.
0036 STOP RUN.
```

Figure 4.7 COBOL program to calculate salesman's commission.

```
TYPE IN PRODUCT CODE Z TO FINISH
A
TYPE IN VALUE OF SALES
100
TYPE IN PRODUCT CODE Z TO FINISH
B
TYPE IN VALUE OF SALES
200
```

```
TYPE IN PRODUCT CODE Z TO FINISH

Z

TOTAL COMMISSION =    ·

025.00
```

Figure 4.8 Sample dialogue for the program in figure 4.7.

Exercise 4.9 Write a simple COBOL program which allows entry of the number of hours worked and the tax rate for an employee, and calculates the net pay, based on a standard pay rate of £10 per hour. Try to improve your program by introducing tax allowance deduction and varying tax rates if you can.

Example 2

This example demonstrates some more sophisticated payroll calculations than were indicated in Exercise 4.9. Payroll is one of the classic applications of sequential file processing, since whenever the payroll program is run, it is necessary to process each employee record in sequence. The program which processes the sequential file in this way is listed in figure 4.10. In order to run the program in figure 4.10, we shall need a file of the appearance of figure 4.11, which we may create using the program in figure 4.12. The latter program provides an 'initialisation' routine which creates the initial file of employee records which will need to be updated later (see example 3.) Some examples of dialogues when the payroll program is run are given in figure 4.13.

```
0001 IDENTIFICATION DIVISION.

0002    PROGRAM-ID. PROG4POINT10.

0003 ENVIRONMENT DIVISION.

0004 INPUT-OUTPUT SECTION.

0005 FILE-CONTROL.

0006 SELECT EMPLOYEES-FILE ASSIGN TO DISK.

0007 DATA DIVISION.

0008 FILE SECTION.

0009 FD EMPLOYEES-FILE

0010 LABEL RECORDS ARE STANDARD

0011 VALUE OF FILE-ID IS "FILE01".
```

```
0012 01 RECORD-1.

0013 02 REF-NO PIC 99.

0014 02 SURNAME PIC A(20).

0015 02 RATE-OF-PAY PIC 99.99.

0016 02 ALLOWANCE PIC 99.

0017 WORKING-STORAGE SECTION.

0018   01 RECORD-1-WS.

0019      02 REF-NO-WS PIC 99.

0020      02 SURNAME-WS PIC A(20).

0021      02 RATE-OF-PAY-WS PIC 99.99.

0022      02 ALLOWANCE-WS PIC 99.

0023   77 E-O-F PIC 9 VALUE IS ZERO.

0024   77 HOURS-WORKED PIC 99.

0025   77 GROSS-PAY PIC 999.99.

0026   77 TAXABLE-PAY PIC 999.99.

0027   77 TAX-PAYABLE PIC 999.99.

0028   77 NET-PAY PIC 999.99.

0029 PROCEDURE DIVISION.

0030 BEGIN.

0031   OPEN INPUT EMPLOYEES-FILE.

0032   READ EMPLOYEES-FILE AT END MOVE 1 TO E-O-F.

0033 PROCESS-EMPLOYEE.

0034   IF E-O-F NOT = 0 GO TO END-OF-FILE.

0035   MOVE RECORD-1 TO RECORD-1-WS.

0036   DISPLAY SURNAME-WS.

0037   DISPLAY "HOW MANY HOURS WORKED".

0038   ACCEPT HOURS-WORKED.

0039   MULTIPLY HOURS-WORKED BY RATE-OF-PAY-WS GIVING
GROSS-PAY.
```

```
0040    SUBTRACT ALLOWANCE-WS FROM GROSS-PAY GIVING
TAXABLE-PAY.

0041    MULTIPLY TAXABLE-PAY BY 0.25 GIVING TAX-
PAYABLE.

0042    SUBTRACT TAX-PAYABLE FROM GROSS-PAY GIVING
NET-PAY.

0043    DISPLAY "NET PAY IS:-".

0044    DISPLAY NET-PAY.

0045    READ EMPLOYEES-FILE AT END MOVE 1 TO E-O-F.

0046    GO TO PROCESS-EMPLOYEE.

0047 END-OF-FILE.

0048    CLOSE EMPLOYEES-FILE.

0049 STOP RUN.
```

Figure 4.10 Program to produce net pay from a payroll file.

Ref	Surname	Hourly rate	Tax allowance

Figure 4.11 Record structure for the payroll program

```
0001 IDENTIFICATION DIVISION.

0002    PROGRAM-ID. PROG4POINT12.

0003 ENVIRONMENT DIVISION.

0004 INPUT-OUTPUT SECTION.

0005 FILE-CONTROL.
```

```
0006 SELECT EMPLOYEES-FILE ASSIGN TO DISK.

0007 DATA DIVISION.

0008 FILE SECTION.

0009 FD EMPLOYEES-FILE

0010 LABEL RECORDS ARE STANDARD

0011 VALUE OF FILE-ID IS "FILE01".

0012    01 RECORD-1.

0013    02 REF-NO PIC 99.

0014    02 SURNAME PIC A(20).

0015    02 RATE-OF-PAY PIC 99.99.

0016    02 ALLOWANCE PIC 99.

0017 WORKING-STORAGE SECTION.

0018    01 RECORD-1-WS.

0019       02 REF-NO-WS PIC 99.

0020       02 SURNAME-WS PIC A(20).

0021       02 RATE-OF-PAY-WS PIC 99.99.

0022       02 ALLOWANCE-WS PIC 99.

0023 PROCEDURE DIVISION.

0024 BEGIN.

0025    OPEN OUTPUT EMPLOYEES-FILE.

0026 NEXT-EMPLOYEE.

0027    DISPLAY "TYPE IN EMPLOYEE NUMBER, 99 TO END".

0028    ACCEPT REF-NO-WS.

0029    IF REF-NO-WS = "99" GO TO END-INPUT.

0030    DISPLAY "TYPE IN EMPLOYEE SURNAME".

0031    ACCEPT SURNAME-WS.

0032    DISPLAY "TYPE IN EMPLOYEE HOURLY RATE".

0033    ACCEPT RATE-OF-PAY-WS.

0034    DISPLAY "TYPE IN EMPLOYEE ALLOWANCES ".
```

```
0035    ACCEPT ALLOWANCE-WS.

0036    WRITE RECORD-1 FROM RECORD-1-WS.

0037    GO TO NEXT-EMPLOYEE.

0038 END-INPUT.

0039    CLOSE EMPLOYEES-FILE.

0040 STOP RUN.
```

Figure 4.12 Program to create the payroll master file for the program in figure 4.10.

Note: If you run the program in figure 4.12 to create the file, you will need to be careful about the exact form of the inputs which you give. In particular, you need to be certain to give a 20-character name, padded out with spaces if necessary. Failure to do this may result in the file containing some residual characters beyond the name typed in.

```
SMITH

HOW MANY HOURS WORKED

10

NET PAY IS :-

035.60

JONES

HOW MANY HOURS WORKED

15

NET PAY IS :-

065.30
```

Figure 4.13 Sample dialogue from running the program in figure 4.10.

Exercise 4.14 Write a simple file processing program which takes a file containing 10 students' names and dates of birth, requests a mark for each person's English A level examination, and produces certificates giving appropriate grades.

Example 3

The ability to update a sequential file by adding extra records, and changing and deleting existing records is central to many data processing applications. The method usually adopted requires the use of a 'transaction' file to update the 'old master' file in order to create a 'new master' file which has the necessary changes incorporated.

It is important in these file updating runs to ensure that the sequence of records in both the transaction file and the old master file is the same. Here we find the COBOL SORT verb extremely useful, since it allows us to create an unsorted transaction file over a period of time, as the changes to be made come to light, and then process it easily to create a sorted transaction file immediately before the main update run. In languages which do not incorporate a built-in sort method, this task would have to be undertaken explicitly by the programmer.

Ref	Surname	Hourly rate	Tax allowance
01	Smith	8.43	47
02	Jones	9.20	51
04	Brown	7.41	43
05	White	6.50	68
08	Black	10.65	32

Figure 4.15   Old master file contents for the payroll program

Ref	Type	Surname	Hourly rate	Tax allowance
02	D			
05	C	*	10.00	*
15	A	Green	8.81	48
04	C	*	*	39

Figure 4.16 Unsorted transaction file for the payroll program.

Ref	Type	Surname	Hourly rate	Tax allowance
02	D			
04	C	*	*	39
05	C	*	10.00	*
15	A	Green	8.81	48

Figure 4.17 Sorted transaction file for the payroll program

Ref	Surname	Hourly rate	Tax allowance
01	Smith	8.43	47
04	Brown	7.41	39
05	White	10.00	68
08	Black	10.65	32
15	Green	8.81	48

Figure 4.18   New master file contents for the payroll program

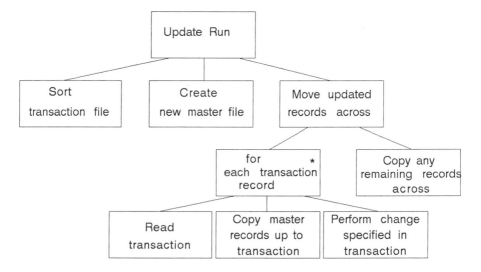

Figure 4.19   Structure diagram illustrating typical sequential file update process.

In this particular example, we shall update the master file of employee data created in example 2 (above). Figures 4.15, 4.16, 4.17 and 4.18 give, respectively, the old master file contents, the unsorted transaction file, the sorted transaction file and the updated master file. Figure 4.19 gives a structure diagram indicating the updating technique and figure 4.20 lists a suitable COBOL program.

```
0001 IDENTIFICATION DIVISION.
0002    PROGRAM-ID. PROG4POINT20.
0003 ENVIRONMENT DIVISION.
0004 INPUT-OUTPUT SECTION.
0005 FILE-CONTROL.
0006 SELECT FILE1 ASSIGN TO DISK.
0007 SELECT FILE2 ASSIGN TO DISK.
0008 SELECT FILET ASSIGN TO DISK.
0009 DATA DIVISION.
0010 FILE SECTION.
0011 FD FILE1
0012 LABEL RECORDS ARE STANDARD
0013 VALUE OF FILE-ID IS "FILE1".
0014    01 RECORD-1.
0015       02 REF-1 PIC 99.
0016       02 SURNAME-1 PIC A(20).
0017       02 HOURLY-RATE-1 PIC 99.99.
0018       02 ALLOWANCE-1 PIC 99.
0019 FD FILE2
0020 LABEL RECORDS ARE STANDARD
0021 VALUE OF FILE-ID IS "FILE2".
0022    01 RECORD-2.
0023       02 REF-2 PIC 99.
0024       02 SURNAME-2 PIC A(20).
```

```
0025        02 HOURLY-RATE-2 PIC 99.99.

0026        02 ALLOWANCE-2 PIC 99.

0027 FD FILET

0028 LABEL RECORDS ARE STANDARD

0029 VALUE OF FILE-ID IS "FILET".

0030   01 RECORD-T.

0031        02 REF-T PIC 99.

0032        02 TRANS-TYPE PIC A.

0033        02 SURNAME-T PIC A(20).

0034        02 HOURLY-RATE-T PIC XXXXX.

0035        02 ALLOWANCE-T PIC XX.

0036 WORKING-STORAGE SECTION.

0037   77 EOF1 PIC 9 VALUE "0".

0038   77 EOFT PIC 9 VALUE "0".

0039   77 MASK PIC X.

0040   01 RECORD-WS.

0041        02 REF-WS PIC 99.

0042        02 SURNAME-WS PIC A(20).

0043        02 HOURLY-RATE-WS PIC 99.99.

0044        02 ALLOWANCE-WS PIC 99.

0045 PROCEDURE DIVISION.

0046 BEGIN.

0047   OPEN INPUT FILE1.

0048   OPEN INPUT FILET.

0049   OPEN OUTPUT FILE2.

0050   READ FILE1 AT END GO TO E-O-F-1.

0051   READ FILET AT END GO TO E-O-F-T.

0052 MORE-1.

0053   IF REF-T > REF-1 PERFORM COPY-ACROSS.
```

```
0054    IF REF-T = REF-1 PERFORM AMEND.

0055    IF REF-T < REF-1 PERFORM INSERT.

0056    GO TO MORE-1.

0057 E-O-F-T.

0058    MOVE 1 TO EOFT.

0059    IF EOF1 = "1" GO TO END-PROGRAM.

0060    PERFORM COPY-ACROSS.

0061    GO TO E-O-F-T.

0062 E-O-F-1.

0063    MOVE 1 TO EOF1.

0064    IF EOFT = "1" GO TO END-PROGRAM.

0065    PERFORM INSERT.

0066    GO TO E-O-F-1.

0067 E-O-F-1A.

0068    MOVE 1 TO EOF1.

0069    READ FILET AT END GO TO E-O-F-T.

0070 COPY-ACROSS.

0071    WRITE RECORD-2 FROM RECORD-1.

0072    READ FILE1 AT END GO TO E-O-F-1.

0073 INSERT.

0074    MOVE REF-T TO REF-WS.

0075    MOVE SURNAME-T TO SURNAME-WS.

0076    MOVE HOURLY-RATE-T TO HOURLY-RATE-WS.

0077    MOVE ALLOWANCE-T TO ALLOWANCE-WS.

0078    WRITE RECORD-2 FROM RECORD-WS.

0079    READ FILET AT END GO TO E-O-F-T.

0080 AMEND.

0081    IF TRANS-TYPE = "D" PERFORM NEXT-RECORD.

0082    IF TRANS-TYPE = "C" PERFORM CHANGE-RECORD.
```

```
0083 CHANGE-RECORD.

0084    MOVE RECORD-1 TO RECORD-WS.

0085    MOVE SURNAME-T TO MASK.

0086    IF MASK NOT = "*" PERFORM CHANGE-NAME.

0087    MOVE HOURLY-RATE-T TO MASK.

0088    IF MASK NOT = "*" PERFORM CHANGE-RATE.

0089    MOVE ALLOWANCE-T TO MASK.

0090    IF MASK NOT = "*" PERFORM CHANGE-ALLOWANCE.

0091    WRITE RECORD-2 FROM RECORD-WS.

0092    PERFORM NEXT-RECORD.

009.3 NEXT-RECORD.

0094    READ FILE1 AT END GO TO E-O-F-1A.

0095    READ FILET AT END GO TO E-O-F-T.

0096 CHANGE-NAME.

0097    MOVE SURNAME-T TO SURNAME-WS.

0098 CHANGE-RATE.

0099    MOVE HOURLY-RATE-T TO HOURLY-RATE-WS.

0100 CHANGE-ALLOWANCE.

0101    MOVE ALLOWANCE-T TO ALLOWANCE-WS.

0102 END-PROGRAM.

0103    CLOSE FILE1.

0104    CLOSE FILE2.

0105    CLOSE FILET.

0106 STOP RUN.
```

Figure 4.20 COBOL program to perform a simple sequential file update.

Example 4

The desire to use file access methods which are not simply sequential but give greater speed to access of individual queries motivates the use of indexed sequential (and other 'direct access') file methods. While a full discussion of these techniques is beyond the scope of this work, it will be useful to gain some insight into the advantages of using COBOL to provide these more complex file structures.

In this example, we consider the use of a simple database of information about the cows on a farm and their milk yields. It will be useful to be able to type a cow's name on a data-entry screen (like that illustrated in figure 4.21) and get the other details about this particular cow.

Cow: Daisy

Milk yield this week: 100 ltrs

Born :   Feb. 1986

Last Calf: Sept   1989

Figure 4.21 Screen display from a direct access file enquiry system

The underlying database is illustrated in figure 4.22, and a very much simplified program to give 'direct' access to the data on Bluebell is illustrated in figure 4.23.

Cow name	Week's yield	Born	Last Calf
Bluebell	108	March 87	May 89
Buttercup	124	Feb 86	June 89
Daisy	104	March 84	May 89

Figure 4.22 Typical records in the milk-yield file

```
0001 IDENTIFICATION DIVISION.
0002   PROGRAM-ID. PROG4POINT23.
0003 ENVIRONMENT DIVISION.
0004 INPUT-OUTPUT SECTION.
0005 FILE-CONTROL.
0006 SELECT COWS ASSIGN TO DISK,
0007 ORGANIZATION IS INDEXED,
0008 ACCESS MODE IS DYNAMIC,
0009 RECORD KEY IS COW-NAME.
0010 DATA DIVISION.
0011 FILE SECTION.
0012 FD COWS
0013 LABEL RECORDS ARE STANDARD,
0014 VALUE OF FILE-ID IS "COWS".
0015   01 RECORD-1.
0016      02 COW-NAME PIC A(15).
0017      02 YIELD PIC 9(4).
0018      02 BORN PIC X(10).
0019      02 LAST-CALF PIC X(10).
0020 WORKING-STORAGE SECTION.
0021 PROCEDURE DIVISION.
0022 BEGIN.
0023   OPEN INPUT COWS.
0024   MOVE "BUTTERCUP" TO COW-NAME.
0025   READ COWS KEY IS COW-NAME.
0026   DISPLAY "COW: " COW-NAME.
0027   DISPLAY "YIELD " YIELD "LTS".
0028   DISPLAY "BORN " BORN.
0029   DISPLAY "LAST CALF " LAST-CALF .
```

```
0030    CLOSE COWS.

0031 STOP RUN.
```

Figure 4.23 A simplified COBOL program which uses Indexed Sequential file organisation.

COBOL's Limitations.

We have identified already the main strength of the COBOL language as being its facilities to process non-numerical data, particularly stored in files and tables. We have also identified the weaknesses of the language as viewed in the 1990's by a programmer:

1) Structure: the COBOL language does not offer the control structures which have come to be expected by today's programmers. It is therefore significantly more difficult to write well designed and structured programs in the COBOL language than in more recently designed alternatives. The maintenance of the resulting COBOL code is also correspondingly more difficult.

2) Discursive style: COBOL programs are long and can be tedious to write.

3) Size of compiler/restriction of implementation: the COBOL language is large and therefore difficult to implement fully on smaller computer systems. It is therefore sometimes the case that implementations of the language available to the programmer do not offer the more advanced features of the language which form the basis for selecting it for the particular application. Two powerful features of the language which are sometimes omitted are the SORT verb, and indexed sequential file processing, both of which are significant in major data processing applications.

The other main limitation of the COBOL language stems from its history as a data processing language. It is therefore inappropriate to attempt to code mathematical and scientific applications using COBOL.

5 Fortran

Introduction

In this chapter, we consider the programming language FORTRAN, one of the earliest high-level programming languages developed, and yet a language still very popular with Mathematical and Scientific programmers.

Background

The FORTRAN programming language was first developed in the late 1950's by IBM workers. It is important for us to remember that the computing world for which the language was originally developed was a very different world from the one with which we are familiar today:

1) At the time when FORTRAN was originally developed, the majority of programming was being undertaken by programmers working in assembly language or machine code. It was essential to persuade potential users of the value of working in a high-level language instead of their accustomed low-level language. They were suspicious that programs compiled from high-level language would be less efficient than those written at low-level, and so were reluctant to take advantage of the easier writing of the programs. The team who designed and implemented the earliest version of FORTRAN were therefore motivated to produce a language which could be implemented efficiently.

This desire resulted in some rather unnatural restrictions being imposed by the language on the user in order to achieve efficiency. We may illustrate one such strange restriction by considering two very similar example programs:

Figure 5.1 lists a simple FORTRAN program which uses a loop to list the squares of the numbers from 1 to 100. Figure 5.2 lists a corresponding program for the squares of the numbers from -10 to +10, but this program would not compile on early FORTRAN implementations since it contravened a requirement that the control variable of a loop must never pass through zero.

```
      PROGRAM SQUAR1
C
C THIS PROGRAM PRINTS A LIST OF THE SQUARES OF NUMBERS
FROM 1 TO 100
C
      INTEGER COUNT,RESULT
      DO 10 COUNT=1,100
      RESULT = COUNT * COUNT
      WRITE(*,20) COUNT,RESULT
   10 CONTINUE
   20 FORMAT('THE SQUARE OF ',I3,' IS ',I6)
      STOP
      END
```

Figure 5.1

```
      PROGRAM SQUAR2
C
C THIS PROGRAM PRINTS A LIST OF THE SQUARES OF NUMBERS
FROM -20 TO 20
C
      INTEGER COUNT,RESULT
      DO 10 COUNT=-20,20
      RESULT = COUNT * COUNT
```

```
      WRITE(*,20) COUNT,RESULT
   10 CONTINUE
   20 FORMAT('THE SQUARE OF ',I3,' IS ',I6)
      STOP
      END
```
Figure 5.2

2) The hardware in use in the late 1950's bore little resemblance to the typical hardware of today. Many early FORTRAN programs were run in single-user mode on a mainframe computer, input and output were by means of punched cards, paper tape and line printers. Graphics (and even lower case letters) were unknown for these early users of the language.

3) The programmers using computers were specialists in their use. Computers were expensive and many of the applications which could afford the use of a computer were industrial, scientific or mathematical. The aspirations of the programmer were therefore directed largely to the solution of mathematical equations and the evaluation of formulae. The ideas of structuring involving the use of procedures were yet to be developed.

FORTRAN became popular because it did provide a realistic and desirable alternative to low-level language programming for mathematical and scientific applications. Its popularity resulted in its being transported outside of its original IBM environment onto other computer systems, but nevertheless some of the limitations on the language which were originally imposed by the IBM environment for which it was initially designed were retained in the versions implemented on rival systems.

By 1966 a standard version of FORTRAN, "FORTRAN IV" or "FORTRAN 66" had emerged, and this standard version was implemented on computer systems until an improved version "FORTRAN 77" was introduced in 1977. FORTRAN 77 was upwards compatible with FORTRAN 66 (which means that FORTRAN 66 programs would run without amendment on FORTRAN 77 systems), but introduced many of the features needed in order to bring the language up to the standards then required by programmers, and also provided the types of facilities necessary in order to utilise the more modern computer systems.

This upgrading of the FORTRAN standard is a continuous process and a new standard is likely to be released shortly by the ANSI X3J3 committee. It is very important that improved standards are released since this removes some of the motivation which would otherwise exist for individual implementors to introduce non-standard extensions to the language in order to satisfy the demands of their users. Such developments are inevitably at the expense of the portability of the programs written using these extensions.

There are disadvantages inherent in the desire to maintain an easy upgrade path by providing upwards compatible versions of a computer language, since it means that the features which allowed programmers in the past to use techniques which are no longer appropriate within the newer situations must be retained. So, for example, improved error checking cannot be introduced if methods used within the older standard would violate the newer checks.

It is also inevitable that a language which has evolved, as FORTRAN has, will be much less well designed than a language which has been designed to suit the present hardware and user situations (as was Pascal in the early 1970's). As an analogy we may contrast the house which is built as a two bedroomed house but is extended in a series of stages to become a five bedroomed house, with the house which is designed and built as a five bedroomed house. Both houses have five bedrooms, but it is likely that the latter will be a more convenient house to live in because it was designed to be the way it is, rather than adapted from a previous version and forced to take account of the previous design.

Why FORTRAN?

FORTRAN stands for FORmula TRANslation, and the name was chosen because that was the original purpose of the language. The early versions of the language were largely restricted to users solving problems of a numerical type. FORTRAN 66 and later versions allowed character processing, but it is not as easy to use as it should be. Some very fast string processing software was developed nevertheless. This makes FORTRAN into a more general-purpose language than it was previously. It would nevertheless be foolhardy to deny that the language's particular strength lies in the evaluation of formulae, and the solution of numerical problems. Within the context of this book, we shall therefore describe FORTRAN as a mathematical or scientific language, while noting that it has the capacity to permit file handling and character handling programs to be written. It might therefore be a very appropriate language for a programmer who was regularly writing scientific applications to undertake an occasional character-based program.

Today, FORTRAN's continued success as a programming language has much to do with history. The language has been accepted as the natural tool for numerical work for over 25 years and therefore there is a large pool of experienced programmers who are committed to the use of FORTRAN and there is also a large pool of library procedures and routines readily available in FORTRAN to undertake some of the more complex programming problems. One of the most important of these is the NAG (Numerical Algorithms Group) library of routines which may be called as subprograms from within a FORTRAN program using a CALL command which passes a number of parameters to the subprogram. (Figure 5.3)

```
      PROGRAM CALLER
C
C THIS PROGRAM CALLS A SUBPROGRAM CONTAINED IN A
SEPARATE FILE
C
      INTEGER A,B,C
      A = 1
      B = 2
      CALL FRED(A,B,C)
      WRITE(*,10)A,B,C
   10 FORMAT('THE SUM OF ',I2,' AND ',I2,' IS ',I2)
      STOP
      END
```

The main program listed above may be compiled separately from the subroutine FRED which it calls. The two files are then combined at the LINK stage.

```
      SUBROUTINE FRED(X,Y,Z)
  C
  C THIS SUBROUTINE ADDS TOGETHER X AND Y AND PUTS THE
  ANSWER IN Z
  C
      INTEGER X,Y,Z
      Z = X + Y
      RETURN
      STOP
      END
```

Figure 5.3

It is probably fair to say that if nobody had ever started using FORTRAN before, then there would be no great movement to use it today, because there are alternatives available which are arguably "better" for the sorts of applications at which FORTRAN is efficient. On the other hand, there has been no great movement away from FORTRAN within the scientific community, because there has so far been no real reason to find an alternative to a language which performs reasonably efficiently at a range of tasks which have changed little over time. FORTRAN has adapted enough to ensure that it has continued to provide the facilities required.

FORTRAN's Facilities

In this section we consider the facilities offered by FORTRAN which make it particularly appropriate for the types of use which we have identified.

1) Data types.

We have become accustomed to languages providing us with different classes of data: in Pascal, for example, we were able to classify numerical data as being either of type integer or of type real. FORTRAN also provides the two data types integer and real, but also provides two additional types for numerical variables. These are the types double precision and complex.

a) Double precision

In order to distinguish between data stored as real and data stored as double precision we shall need to consider for a moment the physical way in which numbers are stored within the computer.

A typical computer might use a 32 bit word length to store the value of a real variable. In other words, the 32 bits are divided into two groups: one group identifies the significant figures of the number represented (the mantissa), while the remainder represent the power of two (the exponent) by which the mantissa should be multiplied in order to give the value represented. Clearly, the greater the number of bits available to represent the mantissa, the greater the degree of accuracy available (i.e. the more significant figures of accuracy) while the greater the number of bits available to represent the exponent, the greater the range of real numbers which may be represented.

Double precision representation involves using two words, rather than one, in which to store the number. The total number of bits available is doubled, and therefore more bits can be made available to represent the mantissa without affecting the range of numbers representable. With double precision representation we may therefore store numbers to a greater number of significant figures.

The benefits gained from the use of double precision representation are at some cost: naturally the amount of memory used to store numbers held in double precision representation is twice that used to store the corresponding real representations, and the time taken to perform calculations and other processing is significantly longer with double precision quantities. Whether or not the use of double precision can be justified will depend upon

i) how much accuracy is required

ii) how much accuracy is offered by the real representation for the FORTRAN implementation in use (for example, word length can vary from 16 bits to 64 bits; real representations using 64 bits give more significant figures than even the double precision from a 16 bit representation).

iii) whether the memory and time losses using double precision representations are acceptable

iv) whether it is meaningful for the values represented to be recorded to the required degree of precision which might justify double precision representation. Simply to store a number to a certain number of digits does not of itself guarantee the accuracy of all the stored digits in the representation. It may therefore be appropriate to use double precision representations of some of the variables involved in calculations in order to improve on the precision of the final answer, without necessarily using double precision throughout the calculation. Figure 5.4 gives an illustration of how this might work out in practice, but the decision as to what degree of accuracy might be expected in the answer to a calculation is not in general straightforward, and is one of the concerns of Numerical Analysts.

Suppose we wish to find the difference between two nearly equal numbers. In this case, if each of the numbers is stored to, say 8 significant figures, then on subtracting we may find that the answer is correct to only, say, 3 significant figures, as this calculation shows:

```
Let A = 1.2345678 and B = 1.2345891

   then B-A = 0.0000213 = 2.13 E -05, to 3 significant
figures.

   If we are able to predict this behaviour in advance,
then we could store A and B in double precision, which
will preserve the accuracy of B-A.
```

Figure 5.4

b) Complex

The complex data type reflects the mathematical basis for the language FORTRAN. Mathematicians often require the use of a representation for the square root of -1, which is generally termed i. A number of the form $x + iy$ which is made up of two parts: the 'real' part x and the 'imaginary' part iy is then known as a complex number. There are techniques available for performing rudimentary arithmetical operations- addition, subtraction, multiplication and division- and various more specialised operations on these complex numbers.

Computer programmers in most computer languages must create their own structures to represent complex numbers and perform the arithmeti-

cal operations explicitly, working from first principles. However FOR-
TRAN reflects its mathematical basis by providing a standard storage
class 'complex' and a set of operators to allow complex arithmetic to be
performed directly (figure 5.5).

Assuming that the variables A,B and C are of type complex and D is
of type REAL, the following examples illustrate the types of operations
permitted.

```
C=A+B
C=A-B
C=A*B
C=A/B
D=AIMAG(A)  (which gives the imaginary part of A)
A=CONJG(B)  (which gives the complex conjugate of B)
```

Figure 5.5

2) Input and Output

The input and output facilities provided by FORTRAN are very
versatile though rather unfriendly to use. They suffer from being based
upon the punched card as the standard input medium and the line printer
as the standard output device and it follows that they derive from the
expectation that both input and output data will best be dealt with 80
columns at a time (a punched card held 80 columns, as did an output
line of many line printers).

The FORMAT statement is used to set up the precise format of the
data referred to in a READ or WRITE statement (figure 5.6)

```
The FORMAT statement allows literal strings to be in-
cluded in output and also the specification of the for-
mat in which data of a particular type is to be input or
output. For example:

I3 specifies an integer variable in 3 digit format.

F8.3 specifies a floating point real representation
of 8 characters, 3 after the decimal point.

E10.4 specifies exponential notation using 10 charac-
```

ters for a real variable, with four digits after the decimal point and one before it in the mantissa and the remaining digits used for the exponent.

The FORMAT statement also allows for the use of files and various other more advanced input/output.

Figure 5.6

3) Predefined functions

Most computer languages provide a range of mathematical functions to evaluate sines, cosines, logarithms and so on. Few can match the range offered by FORTRAN, and several of the more unusual are illustrated in the programs listed in figures 5.7 to 5.9.

```
      PROGRAM BIG
C
C THIS PROGRAM TAKES FOUR INTEGERS FROM THE USER AND PRINTS
C OUT THE BIGGEST
C
      INTEGER A,B,C,D,E
      WRITE(*,30)
      READ(*,10)A,B,C,D
      E=MAX(A,B,C,D)
      WRITE(*,20)A,B,C,D,E
   10 FORMAT(I3,I3,I3,I3)
   20 FORMAT('THE BIGGEST NUMBER OUT OF ',I3,I3,I3,' AND ',I3,' IS ',I3)
   30 FORMAT('TYPE IN FOUR INTEGERS, SEPARATED BY SPACES')
      STOP
      END
```

Figure 5.7

```
       PROGRAM CMPLX
C
C THIS PROGRAM DOES SOME SIMPLE COMPLEX NUMBER ARITH-
METIC
C
       COMPLEX A,B,C
       A=(1.0,2.0)
       B=(2.3,3.4)
       C=A+B
       WRITE(*,10)A,B,C
       A=CONJG(C)
       WRITE(*,20)C,A
       C=SQRT(B)
       WRITE(*,30)B,C
    10 FORMAT('THE SUM OF ',F5.1,F5.1,' AND
 ',F5.1,F5.1,' IS ',F5.1,F5.1)
    20 FORMAT('THE COMPLEX CONJUGATE OF ',F5.1,F5.1,'
 IS ',F5.1,F5.1)
    30 FORMAT('THE COMPLEX SQUARE ROOT OF ',F5.1,F5.1,'
 IS ',F5.1,F5.1)
       STOP
       END
```

Figure 5.8

```
       PROGRAM DBLPRE
C
C THIS PROGRAM ILLUSTRATES SOME SIMPLE DOUBLE PRE-
CISION CALCULATIONS
C
       DOUBLE PRECISION A,B,C
```

```
      A=DLOG10(DBLE(5))
      B=DLOG10(DBLE(3.0))
      C=DEXP(DBLE(4.0))
C THESE ARE THE FS FORTRAN 77 DOUBLE PRECISION FUNC-
TIONS
C FOR LOG AND EXP
      WRITE(*,10)A
      WRITE(*,20)B
      WRITE(*,30)C
      A=B+C
      WRITE(*,40)B,C,A
      A=DPROD(REAL(B),REAL(C))
      WRITE(*,50)B,C,A
   10 FORMAT('THE LOG TO BASE 10 OF 5 IS ',F20.10)
   20 FORMAT('THE LOG TO BASE 10 OF 3 IS ',F20.10)
   30 FORMAT('THE VALUE OF EXP(4) IS ',F20.10)
   40 FORMAT('THE SUM OF ',F20.10,' AND ',F20.10,' IS
 ',F20.10)
   50 FORMAT('THE PRODUCT OF ',F20.10,' AND ',F20.10,'
IS ',F20.10)
      STOP
      END
```

Figure 5.9

4) Functions and Subroutines

FORTRAN 77 responds to the desire of the programmer to define segments of code with a particular purpose by providing the facility to establish functions and subroutines as part of a program.

Functions defined by the programmer are defined either before or after, but never within, the main program or any subprogram. When a function is referenced, the flow of program control passes over to the function, and the values of the arguments listed in the function call are

passed to the parameters in the function definition. The function returns
the value last assigned to a variable by the same name as the function,
before the END of the function is reached (figure 5.10).

```
      PROGRAM EGFUNC
C
C THIS PROGRAM ILLUSTRATES THE USE OF A USER DEFINED
FUNCTION
C
      INTEGER A,B
      WRITE(*,10)
      READ(*,20)A
      B=SQUARE(A)
      WRITE(*,30)B
   10 FORMAT('TYPE IN AN INTEGER')
   20 FORMAT(I3)
   30 FORMAT('THE SQUARE OF THAT INTEGER IS ',I6)
      STOP
      END
      FUNCTION SQUARE(X)
C
C THIS FUNCTION RETURNS THE SQUARE OF ITS INTEGER
ARGUMENT
C
      INTEGER X
      WRITE(*,40)X
      SQUARE=X*X
   40 FORMAT('THE NUMBER PASSED TO THE SQUARE FUNCTION
IS ',I3)
      END
```

Figure 5.10

A simplified situation exists within FORTRAN when a function may be defined using a single statement within the program. In this case we refer to the function as a 'statement function' and the definition of the function may then appear within the main body of the program (figure 5.11).

```
      PROGRAM EGSTFN
C
C THIS PROGRAM ILLUSTRATES THE USE OF A USER DEFINED
STATEMENT FUNCTION
C
      INTEGER A,B
      SQUARE(X)=X*X
      WRITE(*,10)
      READ(*,20)A
      B=SQUARE(A)
      WRITE(*,30)B
   10 FORMAT('TYPE IN AN INTEGER')
   20 FORMAT(I3)
   30 FORMAT('THE SQUARE OF THAT INTEGER IS ',I6)
      STOP
      END
```

Figure 5.11 The use of the statement function in FORTRAN (Note: This program does not compile in FS FORTRAN 77)

A subroutine in FORTRAN corresponds closely with a procedure in Pascal. Once again, it may be used to represent the structure of the solution to a particular problem or to economise on code. Unlike a FORTRAN function, a subroutine CALL need not have any parameters passed to the subroutine, (although any number of parameters may be passed) and no value is returned. Since the parameters are passed as variable parameters, an extra parameter may be used to hold the result of some calculation within the procedure (figure 5.12).

```
      PROGRAM EGSUB1
C
C THIS PROGRAM ILLUSTRATES THE USE OF A SUBROUTINE
WITH PARAMETERS
C INCLUDING A PARAMETER TO RETURN THE RESULT
C
      INTEGER A,B
      WRITE(*,10)
      READ(*,20)A
      CALL SUBSQ(A,B)
      WRITE(*,30)B
   10 FORMAT('TYPE IN AN INTEGER')
   20 FORMAT(I3)
   30 FORMAT('THE SQUARE OF THAT INTEGER IS ',I6)
      STOP
      END
      SUBROUTINE SUBSQ(X,Y)
      INTEGER X,Y
      WRITE(*,40)X
      Y=X*X
      RETURN
   40 FORMAT('THE NUMBER PASSED TO X WAS ',I3)
      END
```

Figure 5.12

FORTRAN functions and arrays may be used by the programmer to
provide the types of mathematical operations on vectors and matrices
which are commonly required (figure 5.13).

```
    PROGRAM MATRIX
  C
  C THIS PROGRAM READS IN TWO ROWS OF TWO INTEGERS TO A
2x2 MATRIX
  C AND THEN MULTIPLIES THE MATRIX BY ITSELF
  C
      DIMENSION MAT1(2,2),MAT2(2,2)
      WRITE(*,10)
      READ(*,20)MAT1(1,1),MAT1(1,2)
      READ(*,20)MAT1(2,1),MAT1(2,2)
      CALL MATMLT(MAT1,MAT2)
      WRITE(*,30)
      WRITE(*,40)MAT2(1,1),MAT2(1,2)
      WRITE(*,40)MAT2(2,1),MAT2(2,2)
   10 FORMAT('TYPE IN TWO ROWS OF TWO INTEGERS')
   20 FORMAT(I3,I3)
   30 FORMAT('HERE IS THE PRODUCT OF THAT MATRIX WITH
ITSELF')
   40 FORMAT(' [',I3,' ',I3,']')
      STOP
      END
      SUBROUTINE MATMLT(M1,M2)
      DIMENSION M1(2,2),M2(2,2)
      DO 70 I=1,2
      DO 60 J=1,2
      M2(I,J)=0
      DO 50 K=1,2
      M2(I,J)=M2(I,J)+M1(I,K)*M1(K,J)
   50 CONTINUE
```

```
60 CONTINUE
70 CONTINUE
   RETURN
   END
```

Figure 5.13

Note: Figure 5.13 introduces the fundamental looping construction of FORTRAN- the DO loop. This is almost identical to the BASIC FOR..NEXT loop which allows for a set of statements to be repeated while a counter varies between a starting value and a finishing value at a specified step interval. Thus

```
FOR I = 1 TO 21 STEP 4 ... NEXT I
```

in BASIC, corresponds to the FORTRAN

```
DO 100 I = 1,21,4 ... 100 CONTINUE
```

FORTRAN Applications

We have already identified the main areas of FORTRAN applications as being mathematical and scientific. In this section, we shall look briefly at three typical scientific computer programs and indicate how FORTRAN's facilities may be used in this area.

Example 1

In the first example program, we illustrate the simple problem of solving a quadratic equation. The equation $ax^2 + bx + c = 0$ has solutions given by the formula $x = (-b + b^2 - 4ac)/2a$ and a program to apply this formula is given in figure 5.14. The advantage of using FORTRAN for solving this particular problem lies in the natural availability of the COMPLEX data type which saves the programmer a substantial amount of effort. In order to illustrate the advantage over Pascal which provides no such complex data type, a corresponding program in Pascal is shown in figure 5.15.

```
PROGRAM QUAD
C
C THIS PROGRAM SOLVES A QUADRATIC EQUATION WITH
INTEGER
C COEFFICIENTS, INCLUDING THE USE OF COMPLEX ROOTS
C
      REAL DISC
      INTEGER A,B,C
      COMPLEX X1,X2,SQT,CPDISC
      WRITE(*,10)
      READ(*,20)A
      READ(*,20)B
      READ(*,20)C
      DISC=REAL(B*B-4*A*C)
      CPDISC=CMPLX(DISC,0.0)
      SQT=CSQRT(CPDISC)
C THE SQUARE ROOT USED HERE GIVES A COMPLEX RESULT
      X1 = (-1*B+SQT)/(2*A)
      X2 = (-1*B-SQT)/(2*A)
      WRITE(*,30)X1
      WRITE(*,40)X2
   10 FORMAT('TYPE IN COEFFICIENTS A,B,C ON SEPARATE
LINES')
   20 FORMAT(I3)
   30 FORMAT('THE ROOTS OF THE EQUATION ARE
(',F3.1,',',F3.1,')')
   40 FORMAT('AND (',F3.1,',',F3.1,')')
      STOP
      END
```

Figure 5.14 (This program does not run in FS FORTRAN 77)

```
program quadratic(input,output);
type
  solution = record
      realpart:real;
      imagpart:real
      end;
var
a,b,c:integer;
disc,root:real;
x1,x2:solution;
begin
writeln('Type in the coefficients a, b, and c or
separate lines');
readln(a);
readln(b);
readln(c);
disc:=b*b-4*a*c;
root:=sqrt(abs(disc));
if disc<0 then
  begin
  x1.realpart:=-1*b/(2*a);
  x2.realpart:=x1.realpart;
  x1.imagpart:=root/(2*a);
  x2.imagpart:=-1*x1.imagpart
  end
else
  begin
  x1.realpart:=(-1*b+root)/(2*a);
  x2.realpart:=(-1*b-root)/(2*a);
```

```
    x1.imagpart:=0;

    x2.imagpart:=0

 end;

 writeln('The    two    roots    are    (',x1.real-
part:4:2,',',x1.imagpart:4:2,')');

 writeln('and    (',x2.realpart:4:2,',',x2.im-
agpart:4:2,')')

    end.
```

Figure 5.15

Exercise 5.16 Try to rewrite program 5.14 to allow for the solution of the same quadratic equation but allowing for the values of a, b and c to be complex. (Hint: the same formula applies).

Example 2

Numerical analysis is a second major application area for the FORTRAN language, and here the use of double precision numbers for calculations can result in greatly improved accuracy in the final results. In this example the trapezium rule is used to approximate the area under the curve $y = x^2$ between the values x=0 and x=3 (figures 5.17 and 5.18). The program gives the values for the integral, taking successively smaller slices (corresponding to decreasing the value of h). Since mathe-

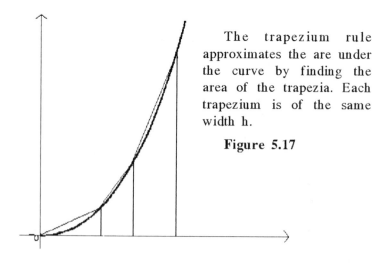

The trapezium rule approximates the are under the curve by finding the area of the trapezia. Each trapezium is of the same width h.

Figure 5.17

maticians are able to calculate the true value exactly, we are able to find the errors in the approximate values calculated by the program. These errors are represented in figure 5.19.

```
      PROGRAM TRAP
C
C THIS PROGRAM EVALUATES THE INTEGRAL OF X SQUARED
FROM X=0 TO X=3
C USING THE TRAPEZIUM RULE AND VARYING WIDTH STRIPS.
C
      DOUBLE PRECISION X,Y,INTEG,H,ERROR
      INTEGER STEPS,COUNT
      DO 20 STEPS = 3,81,3
      H = 3.0/STEPS
      INTEG = 0.0
      DO 10 COUNT = 1,STEPS-1
      X=COUNT*H
      Y=X*X
      INTEG=INTEG+Y*H
   10 CONTINUE
      INTEG=INTEG+0*0*H/2+3*3*H/2
      ERROR=INTEG-9.0
      WRITE(*,30)H,INTEG,ERROR
   20 CONTINUE
   30 FORMAT('H=',F16.12,' INTEGRAL=',F16.12,'
ERROR=',F18.12)
      STOP
      END
```

Figure 5.18

This table represents the first few values in the output from the program in figure 5.18.

H	INTEGRAL	ERROR
1.000000000000	9.500000000000	.500000000000
0.500000000000	9.125000000000	.12500000000
0.333333333333	9.055554115110	.055554115110
0.250000000000	9.031250000000	.031250000000
0.199999988079	9.019998494387	.019998494387

Figure 5.19 The error becomes smaller as the value of H becomes smaller.

Exercise 5.20 Repeat the program in figure 5.18 but changing all the variables to real instead of double precision. What is the effect on the accuracy of the answers?

Example 3

Our third example is also taken from the numerical solution of equations. Newton's method for solving the equation $f(x) = x^2 - 2 = 0$ gives the iteration $x(n+1) = x(n) - f(x(n))/f'(x(n)) = x(n) - (x(n)^2 - 2)/(2x(n)) = x(n)/2 + 1/x(n)$.

An iteration method allows us to generate successive approximations to the true value (which is in this case the square root of 2). The Newton method will converge for this iteration, and we may obtain any required degree of accuracy simply by continuing with the method until successive approximations are sufficiently close together.

The implementation of the Newton technique for the present example is listed in figure 5.21.

```
PROGRAM NEWTON

C

C THIS  PROGRAM  EVALUATES  AN  APPROXIMATION  TO  THE
SQUARE

C ROOT OF 2 BY NEWTON'S METHOD

C
```

```
      REAL APP1,APP2
      INTEGER N
      APP1=1
      APP2=1
      N=0
   10 APP1=APP2
      WRITE(*,20)N,APP1
      N=N +1
      APP2=APP1/2+1/APP1
      IF (ABS(APP1-APP2).GT.0.002) GO TO 10
C THE CONDITION HERE GOVERNS THE ACCURACY OF THE
FINAL APPROXIMATION
   20 FORMAT('ITERATIONS ',I6,' APPROX = ',F20.18)
      STOP
      END
```

Figure 5.21

Exercise 5.22 Repeat the method of the program in figure 5.21, but change the degree of accuracy demanded within your programs and note the number of iterations which are needed in each case. (The degree of accuracy demanded by the program presented here was 0.002. Try 0.001 and 0.005, for example.) What do you notice about the way in which the error size tolerated is related to the number of iterations required?

FORTRAN's limitations

As we have discussed already, FORTRAN is a language which has developed over a thirty year period to suit the needs of FORTRAN programmers who are engaged mainly in mathematical and scientific programming. It is therefore unreasonable to list as limitations the inability to perform operations which the language was never intended to include. In this section we shall confine ourselves to identifying those aspects of the FORTRAN language which fail to satisfy adequately the mathematical and scientific communities.

1) Looping constructions

We have identified in earlier chapters the three principal looping constructions which are commonly offered by programming languages. The count-controlled loop is represented in FORTRAN by means of the DO statement which we encountered in the example program in figure 5.19. The remaining two types of loop are both condition-controlled loops, which may have the checking of the condition at the beginning of the loop (as with the WHILE construction in Pascal) or at the end of the loop (as with the REPEAT...UNTIL construction in Pascal). FORTRAN does not support either condition-controlled loop directly, although either may of course be constructed by the programmer by using IF statements and jumps, as was necessary in the program in figure 5.21. The relevant section of that program is reproduced here as figure 5.23.

```
10 APP1=APP2
   WRITE(*,20)N,APP1
   N=N+1
   APP2=APP1/2+1/APP1
   IF (ABS(APP1-APP2).GT.0.002) GO TO 10
```

Figure 5.23

The absence of condition-controlled loops in FORTRAN is seen as a limitation by programmers today since it inhibits the writing of well-designed structured programs. The almost unavoidable use of jumps within programs may encourage the production of the type of programs described by some as 'spaghetti-programs,' where the route taken through the program's code is in such a muddle as to resemble a plate of spaghetti!

2) The inconvenience of Input/Output

Considering how often programmers require the use of simple input/output facilities, it is surprising how frequently we identify this as an unsatisfactory area within programming languages. The root of the problem so far as the FORTRAN language is concerned, lies in the retention of the FORMAT statement which was ideal for describing the way in which data was to be provided for the program in the form of a stack of punched cards. Here we may see the tension which exists between, on the one hand, the desire to provide new versions of an older computer language which retain familiar statements and allow programmers with previous experience in the language to adapt quickly to the new version, while on the other hand, the new situation might make changes to the methods used appropriate.

To illustrate the complexity of managing FORTRAN input/output, the program listed in figure 5.24 is a simple program which will accept two real numbers as input and which outputs their product. As may be readily observed, apart from the awkwardness of the FORMAT statement, the program is extremely straightforward.

```
      PROGRAM PRODCT

C

C THIS PROGRAM ACCEPTS TWO REAL NUMBERS AND OUTPUTS
THEIR PRODUCT

C REAL A,B,C

      WRITE(*,10) READ(*,20)A

      READ(*,20)B

      C=A*B

      WRITE(*,30)C

   10 FORMAT('TYPE IN TWO REAL NUMBERS, ONE PER LINE')

   20 FORMAT(F10.5)

   30 FORMAT('THEIR PRODUCT IS ',F10.5)

      STOP

      END
```

Figure 5.24

6 C

Introduction

In this chapter, we discuss the programming language C, which has become popular recently for a wide variety of programming applications.

Background

The programming language C was created by Dennis Ritchie of Bell Labs in 1972. Ritchie was working alongside Ken Thompson at the time, designing the UNIX operating system. C itself was derived from Thompson's earlier language 'B'.

C may be distinguished from other languages by its chief design goal: to be a tool for working programmers, and therefore useful. Thus, we may contrast the *elegance* of Pascal, the *simplicity* of writing elementary programs using BASIC and the *usefulness* of C. C is rapidly becoming one of the most popular and widely used programming languages for the development of applications. It is flexible, convenient, powerful and efficient. C is also portable, although, for reasons which we shall discuss later, programs written in C are likely to be a little less portable than their Pascal counterparts.

C is a modern language which reflects present day thinking about the design of well-written programs. C therefore provides the comprehensive range of control structures needed to allow well-structured programs to be written. Its design by programmers for programmers is reflected in the facility to write very compact code in C. In other words, the actual statements which need to be written in order to perform a given operation in C are significantly shorter (take fewer typing strokes) than the corresponding instructions in many other languages. C provides simple short ways to express the types of operations which are frequently required by programmers. The disadvantage of this compact source code lies in the relative unreadability of C source code when compared to more discursive languages such as Pascal. For experienced C programmers, however, C source code is very readable.

C does not behave as a typical 'high-level' language, because it offers a number of features which are more normally associated with 'low-level' languages such as assembly language. These include the ability to write data to and from particular memory addresses, facilities for operations on the contents of memory locations, and instructions for incrementing and decrementing integer variables - these C instructions correspond exactly with machine code instructions and are therefore translated quickly and economically into the equivalent machine code. These facilities allow the experienced C programmer to maintain full control over the method which the computer will use to perform a particular task- rather as would the assembly language programmer-while having the benefits which accrue from working in a fundamentally high-level language development environment. Thus C allows the programmer the flexibility and efficiency of working at low level with the advantages of working at high-level, for example the more advanced data structures and program flow controls typical of today's computer languages. For this reason, C is sometimes described as a 'high-level low-level language' or as a 'low-level high-level language'.

The C language is widely available on a variety of different computer architectures. Originally C was developed alongside the UNIX operating system and was therefore used in a predominantly mini-computer environment. Now the desire to offer UNIX on other architectures-notably the more powerful microcomputers-has provided motivation to develop C compilers for these systems. UNIX has been written in C, and therefore a simple way to install UNIX on a particular system is to use a C compiler to compile UNIX for that particular system.

We remarked earlier that C programs were portable. This is because versions of C have been designed to follow reasonably closely a standard definition described in the book 'The C programming language' by

B.W.Kernighan and D.M.Ritchie (1978), which has now been superseded by a draft ANSI standard for the C language, proposed by the X3J11 standard committee of ANSI. Unfortunately, it is in the nature of the types of facilities on offer with the C language, that the low-level features are likely to be machine specific, and this limits portability somewhat, even among implementations which adhere rigidly to the standard. We shall see later how these incompatibilities can be largely avoided by the use of library facilities.

C was not originally designed with the writing of applications programs in mind, but rather for the ease of development of systems programs in a high-level language environment. For this reason, the language is at its weakest when we consider the facilities offered appropriate to applications programs. The most notable weakness is in the lack of any input/output routines.

Input/Output is an area in which most high-level languages are strong and offer a variety of facilities. We were able to identify the absence of anything more than rudimentary input/output facilities in Pascal as a major weakness of that language and it might be expected that the absence of any I/O facilities in C would be a similar weakness. Paradoxically, this has not proved to be the case. In the absence of any defined standard of input/output, it has been left up to the implementors of the language to define their own. This has resulted in the facility for C to be adapted to suit the needs of the customer in a much more flexible way than would have been possible otherwise. Unfortunately, however, this has the natural consequence that different implementations have incompatible input/output facilities.

Programmers who use the C language from within a UNIX operating system are provided with a Standard I/O library of facilities which come with the operating system and may be used from within the C program (Figure 6.1). These users have the advantage that the library will be defined with the same functions available regardless of the particular UNIX implementation in use. Following on from this, it has become usual for other versions of C to be provided in two parts:

1) the language itself: this allows the programmer to write programs, but the programs are unable to talk to anyone or relate to anything outside the program

2) a library of routines which are essential to allow the programs

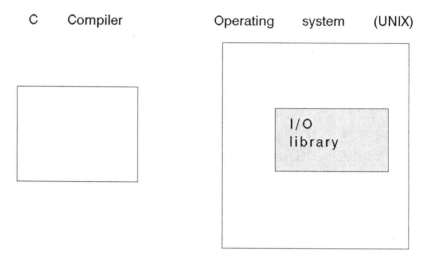

Figure 6.1 The UNIX operating system comes with an I/O library which the C compiler may use

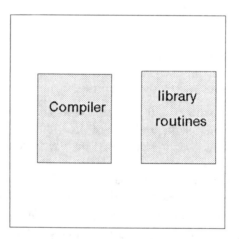

Figure 6.2 A typical C compiler is provided together with a library of essential routines

developed to communicate with the outside world. (Figure 6.2)

These libraries must be developed separately for each particular implementation of C. In the past there has been no standard definition of these libraries, and it has therefore been normal for different C implementations to come equipped with broadly similar but nevertheless incompatible libraries of facilities for input/output. Theoretically, the individual programmer could write additional library routines, but these would also have to be rewritten for different implementations and would typically need to be developed in assembly language.

In recognition of the importance of the provision of a standard set of library functions for use alongside C compilers, the draft ANSI standard includes a specification of the library functions which must be supplied for a 'hosted' environment. A 'hosted' environment is one which provides libraries while a 'non-hosted' environment is one which does not.

The reader may question the value of 'non-hosted' environments since these will not allow communication with the outside world. The users of these non-hosted environments would typically be writing programs for embedded systems like washing machine controllers or for computer firmware which have no need for conventional computer input/output interfaces (Figure 6.3).

HOSTED	NON-HOSTED
Provides libraries	No libraries
Conventional applications programs	Specialised applications, such as domestic appliance controllers which do not use the normal I/O

Figure 6.3

Programming with C

Having discussed the underlying design aims for the C language, it is appropriate for us to turn our attention to look at some C computer programs and examine how the design aims are reflected in the program structure and statements.

As a preliminary example, the program in figure 6.4 produces the words 'Hello, this is your computer speaking' displayed on the screen.

```
#include <stdio.h>
main()
{
printf("Hello, this is your computer speaking");
}
```

Figure 6.4

The overall structure of this program is clear to see. It consists of the single function main which is described by the statements enclosed within the brackets { and }. We shall see in the example programs that every C program is made up of a number of functions, one of which is always known as main. It is the function main which is executed when the program is run, and all the other functions defined within the program will execute as they are called by the function main.

We have previously found it appropriate to distinguish, for most languages, between functions and procedures. Functions have always hitherto produced some result which could then be assigned to a particular variable or used in output, while procedures provided a means of executing a series of language statements. For both functions and procedures, it has often been possible to define local variables and to pass parameters. In C, the distinction between functions and procedures is not made explicitly. Instead, all these collections of statements are grouped to form functions, but functions may or may not return an actual result. Thus we have functions which return no value (or *void* functions) which correspond exactly with our previous notion of procedures, and functions which return a value and correspond to the functions which we have previously understood.

In ANSI C, void functions will be identified by the use of the word 'void' in their function declaration whereas in the Kernighan and Ritchie standard, the absence of a type for the value returned indicated that the function was void. Figure 6.5 gives examples to illustrate the two standards.

```
fred()
{
/* statements within the body of function fred */
}
```

Figure 6.5a The Kernighan and Ritchie standard

```
void fred(void)
{
/* statements within the body of function fred */
}
```

Figure 6.5b The draft ANSI standard

Returning to our consideration of figure 6.4, we may identify the program as being in two parts.

The first part of the program: the statement

```
#include<stdio.h>
```

is a preprocessor directive. Our earlier discussion highlighted input and output as being two fundamental processes which are always included in a hosted C implementation by means of added library routines. Since the present example requires the use of output, we need to instruct the C system to include the standard input/output facilities given by the 'header file' stdio.h. '#include' is the statement which we shall use to include such library header files, and is a directive to the preprocessor- a text manipulation utility provided as part of the C system which incorporates the required library routines within the source code prior to the action of the compiler.

Technically, the effect of the #include statement is that the preprocessor will replace that line in the source code with the entire contents of the file stdio.h.

The remainder of figure 6.4 consists of the definition of the function main. Notice the empty brackets after the word main. This reflects the fact that the function will be called without passing any parameter values. The { and } within the function correspond exactly to the begin and end around the body of a function in Pascal, for example, and serve simply to delimit the statements which together make up the function.

The printf function used within the function main is defined within the library file stdio.h. In theory at least, the program as given in figure 6.4 would fail if the #include statement were omitted, because the C compiler would be unaware of the definition of the function printf. In practice, some C systems are tolerant of this particular omission and assume the inclusion of stdio.h if necessary. The ANSI standard demands the inclusion of the #include statement within the program.

Figure 6.6 illustrates the use of two functions. The function outinfo is void (returning no value) and behaves as a procedure would in other languages. The function ininfo takes in the integer value typed in by the operator and returns it as the function value. The return instruction defines the value to be returned by the function. The function main consists of function calls to the other two functions.

Notice that the C language demands the declaration of variables. We have declared the variables i,j to be of type integer before the start of the function main. In a similar way to that used in Pascal, we may declare local variables within a particular function, and these variables would be available only within that function. To provide an additional flexibility, we may also define variables to be 'static'. When we define a static variable within a particular function, the value is still available only within that function, but in this case, the value is retained on exiting from the function, and will become available again next time the function is entered. The more normal 'automatic' allocation of local variables results in the value being destroyed each time the function is left.

```
#include <stdio.h>
int i,j;
main()
{
void outinfo(void);
```

```
int ininfo(void);
/* these are the declarations of the functions
defined later*/
i = ininfo();
j = i * 2;
outinfo();
}
void outinfo(void)
{
printf(" when you double %d you get %d\n",i,j);
}
int ininfo(void)
{
printf("Please type in a whole number\n");
scanf("%d",&i);
return(i);
}
```

Figure 6.6

The program listed in figure 6.6 introduces the scanf function from within the header file stdio.h. The scanf function provides a means of inputting data from the keyboard, but must be recognised as being both more versatile and more complicated to use than the corresponding instructions found in other high-level languages (such as INPUT in Basic or readln in Pascal). The scanf function call within the function ininfo which we have declared in the example has two arguments. The first argument gives details of the form of the input expected. Thus %d refers to the fact that the user of the program is expected to type in a decimal integer, and therefore the characters typed in should be interpreted and stored in this light. The second argument gives the address where the value is to be stored.

It is important to contrast the situations represented by the `printf` function which accepts the *identifier* of the variable as the argument, and the scanf function which accepts the *address* in storage where the variable is to be located. The programmer needs to be careful to ensure that the correct parameter is given in each case. This is simple since C provides the qualifiers & and * to assist conversion between a location and its address (as can be seen from figure 6.7). There is no intrinsic disadvantage in using functions which take the address of a variable as their argument, and indeed we shall see shortly how this gives us additional flexibility, but the inconsistency identified here between two closely related functions can prove inconvenient.

```
Contents          Address in memory
fred              &fred
*sam              sam
```

Figure 6.7

Note In the scanf statement we are required to give information about the form of input to the computer. Thus the user input of '123' can be interpreted as a string of 3 character, as a single integer, or even as 123 hex. The scanf statement can be used to store any of these three representations in a particular memory location, and each will take a different form. This is symptomatic of a general tendency within C to allow the user the flexibility to store different types of variable within the same variable location, and leads C to be a weakly typed language. This flexibility brings with it the danger that no error report will be given if the programmer makes a mistake!

Exercise 6.8 Write a program in C which accepts the values of three integer variables number1, number2 and number3 and prints out their sum.

Routine features of C

It should come as no surprise to the reader that C supports arrays, loops, and various decision-making constructions. These will not be discussed in detail here, but will be used in the example programs as appropriate.

Some more advanced features

1) Macros

The use of a macro, which involves using an abreviation to represent a longer section of C source code, is allowed by the #define directive. The effect of #define is simply to instruct the preprocessor to replace any reference to the defined macro within the source code by its extended version. The use of macros can assist in the production of relatively easy to read source code, and can also keep the original source shorter. (Figures 6.9a and 6.9b)

```c
#define TITLE printf(" Here is the standard title")
main()
{
function1();
function2();
function3();
}
function1()
{
TITLE;
printf("This is function 1");
}
function2()
{
TITLE;
printf("This is function 2");
}
```

```
function3()
{
TITLE;
printf("This is function 3");
}
```

Figure 6.9a The use of a macro to define the title for repeated use.

```
main()
{
function1();
function2();
function3();
}
function1()
{
printf(" Here is the standard title");
printf("This is function 1");
}
function2()
{
printf(" Here is the standard title");
printf("This is function 2");
}
function3()
{
printf(" Here is the standard title");
printf("This is function 3");
}
```

Figure 6.9b Program corresponding to figure 6.9a without using a macro definition.

2) Separate Compilation of separate sections of a file

One of the features of C which we have already used is the inclusion of standard libraries of functions. A set of these libraries would normally be included with each C implementation, and in fact a particular specification for standard libraries which should be provided alongside the compiler is defined in the draft ANSI standard for C. It is also possible for the C programmer to develop his own collection of library functions which may then be included in programs from within a header file using the #include preprocessor command.

Figure 6.10a gives an example of a header file which produces a particular form of output and figure 6.10b gives a program which uses the header file from figure 6.10a.

```
/* Fancy output header file fancy.h */
#include <stdio.h>
fancyout(c)
char c;
{
printf("****%c****",c);
}
```

Figure 6.10a The header file fancy.h for use in program 6.10b

```
#include<a:fancy.h>
main()
{
fancy("x");
}
```

Figure 6.10b This program uses the header file fancy.h from figure 6.10a

The #include command instructs the preprocessor to include the contents of the header file specified in place of the #include statement. Thus, the compiler simply behaves as though the contents of the header file had been included within the program listing (figure 6.11). It is therefore equivalent to the programmer inserting the contents of the header file into the program source code prior to compilation.

```
#include <stdio.h>
fancyout(c)
char c;
{
printf("****%c****",c);
}
main()
{
fancy("x");
}
```

Figure 6.11 After the preprocessor acts upon the #include instruction in figure 6.10b, the effective source listing is like this.

While this may be a convenient way to include additional functions without making the source code excessively large, C also provides an additional feature, through the use of the linking process, which does not require that the source code segments are combined in this way but instead allows for the development of the program in a modular way.

This additional feature of C is facilitated (within C) by the extern command which allows for variables to be defined in one part of a program and used in another and by the linking (within the operating environment) of independently written and compiled source files into a single executable program. Each file containing part of the complete program is compiled separately, and then all the files required are linked after the compilation. A special command is given which lists all the different program files and library files which are to be combined. This is one of the features of C which has made it particularly suitable for the development of large programs since the separate sections of the program may be developed independently. (Figure 6.12)

This approach has several advantages:

i) each of the files containing function definitions may be debugged separately prior to the final combination of all the necessary sections to make the complete program.

ii) programs may be developed in a modular way, perhaps with different programmers working on different files of function descriptions.

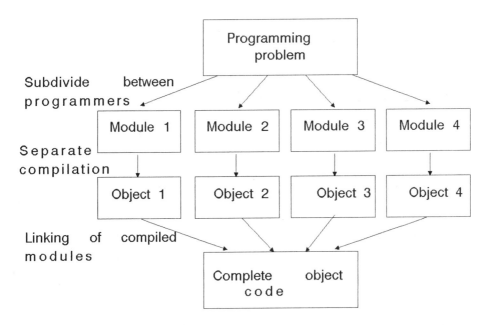

Figure 6.12 Modular development of a C program

iii) Only those files which have been altered since the previous compilation need to be recompiled at each stage. This may enhance compilation speed quite markedly.

iv) As with all other modular approaches to programming, it is likely that changes to the completed program may be confined to the contents of a small number of relatively small files of source code rather than having to make changes to the whole program.

Figure 6.13a gives a program listing which has been subdivided into two files and figure 6.13b lists the instructions for compiling and linking the files to produce an executable program in the C implementation *Zortech C.*

```
/* This is the contents of file1.c */
main()
{
function1();
```

```
function2();
function3();
}
/* This is the contents of file2.c */
#include <stdio.h>
function1()
{
printf("Function 1");
}
function2()
{
printf("Function 2");
}
function3()
{
printf("Function 3");
}
```

Figure 6.13a The program has been segmented into two files - file1.c and file2.c

```
zc1 file1.c
zc2 file1.c
zc1 file2.c
zc2 file2.c
link c + file1 + file2 , file1, file1, nl
```

Figure 6.13b

The program from figure 6.13a must be compiled and linked. The details of the commands necessary will vary for different C implementations, but the need to specify separate compilations (in two stages in this case) for each file, followed by a linking of the object codes is typical.

2) Add-on Libraries

We have identified already the importance of one particular C library 'stdio.h' which provides all the standard routines required to provide for input and output of data within C programs. The widespread adoption of C as a programming language for the development of applications programs has resulted in a large number of other libraries of functions being developed by various software suppliers. This means that, within most C environments, it is possible for the programmer to purchase ready-made functions which perform a variety of tasks and which may then be incorporated within the programmer's own programs.

It is important to distinguish here between the library of functions which may be purchased and then incorporated in the programmer's work without further licence charge, and the package of additional functions which would then need to be licenced to every user of the programs developed. The financial implications of the latter approach are such as to make the use of libraries uneconomic unless the licence permits the distribution of software including the library functions. This is in fact almost always the case.

Typically these additional libraries are incorported by means of a #include directive within the programmer's own program, and the software company usually supplies the source code for the library to allow for limited tailoring by the programmer to suit his individual needs. Alternatively, object code libraries may be incorporated within the link phase of code generation in a similar way to the linking of sections of program developed in separate files. Recent libraries developed have included routines for making user-friendly environments- providing the facilities to produce pull-down menus- and various sophisticated input facilities with specialised error trapping.

An advantage to the programmer of using these ready-written libraries is that a professional-looking product can be written more quickly, and more reliably so long as the library is reliably tested before purchase. Software packages developed by different programmers can be given the same overall appearance by the use of the same standard libraries. This may be seen as an advantage (to a large company which employs several programmers on related projects) or a disadvantage (to a programmer who is prevented from stamping his own personality on the program.) It also becomes rather easier to produce software which runs under a variety of operating systems and screen displays when the same add-on library is available for each operating system/display combination. Although not initially cheap, the speed and reliability of software development using these add-on libraries is sufficient to justify their cost to most C programmers.

Figure 6.14 shows how the comparison between writing the entire program and using libraries might work out in practice.

3) Pointer variables and parameters

One of the most powerful aspects of the C language is the way in which the programmer is given the flexibility to make the computer behave in the precise way required in a particular situation. One of the ways in which this is done is to use two methods of addressing data accessed within the computer program.

For example, in a C program, the value 100 may be stored in a particular location called Fred. Fred is then the identifier of the storage location, and the use of the identifier Fred will always relate within that part of the program to the same storage location.

On the other hand, we may use a *pointer* to a storage location. Thus we may, for example, define Sam to be a pointer to a storage location and then make Sam point to the storage location occupied by the 100 (i.e. Sam points to the storage location occupied by Fred). In this case a reference to the identifier Sam gives us access to the current value stored in the location Sam- i.e. the address of the place in memory that Sam currently points to. Thus at present, *Sam gives access to the value stored within the variable Fred. But Sam is a variable pointer, which may therefore be changed to point at a different memory location later. Thus *Sam will not necessarily always access the contents of the same variable (figure 6.15).

In Pascal we met the distinction between variable and value parameters. When we accessed a function or procedure we were able to pass variables into that function/procedure in two essentially different ways.

i) when the variable is passed in as a value parameter, only the value of the variable is taken on by the parameter. In other words, the parameter contains an additional copy of the original variable value and on return from the procedure/function, the variable retains its original value. Therefore any statements within the body of the procedure/function

Add-on library use	Specially written procedures
Cost of puchasing library. Possible cost of licences for each user of the software.	Time spent on developing procedures. Time spent on debugging.

Figure 6.14 Comparison of costs for developing software with or without the use of an add-on library

which affected the value of the parameter have no affect on the value of the variable (figure 6.16).

ii) when a variable parameter is used, the actual variable address is passed over to the function/procedure and so there is only one copy of the variable referred to. Changes made to the parameter within the function/procedure are therefore made to the actual variable, which does not return to its original value on exiting from the function/procedure (figure 6.17).

Now that we have discussed pointers in relation to C programming, we may see in a little more detail exactly what is happening inside Pascal when we use these two types of parameter.

In a Pascal program, a call to a function/procedure with a value parameter is straightforward. A new location is set up which contains the value which is passed as the parameter and this location is referenced by the parameter identifier within the function/procedure. When the program exits from the function/procedure, the extra memory location is discarded, and clearly if a variable was used to specify the value of the parameter, its value would be unaffected.

On the other hand, when a variable parameter is used, a *new* storage location is established which contains the address of the original variable (i.e. a pointer to the original variable). Whenever the parameter identifier

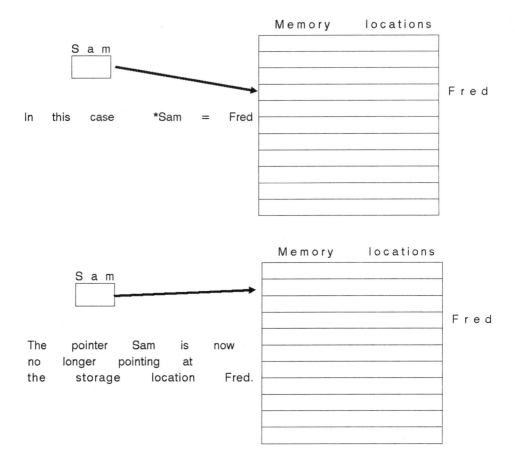

Figure 6.15

is used, the address of the *original* variable is found and changes are made to the original copy of the variable. On leaving the function/procedure, the additional location containing the address of the variable parameter is discarded, but any changes made to the parameter will be permanent. The difference between the operation of a value parameter and a variable parameter in Pascal is therefore that with a variable parameter it is the value of a pointer which is passed to the function/procedure, whereas with a value parameter, it is the value of the variable (figure 6.18).

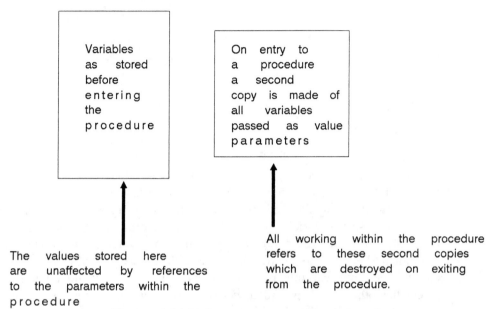

The values stored here are unaffected by references to the parameters within the procedure

All working within the procedure refers to these second copies which are destroyed on exiting from the procedure.

Figure 6.16 Value parameter operation

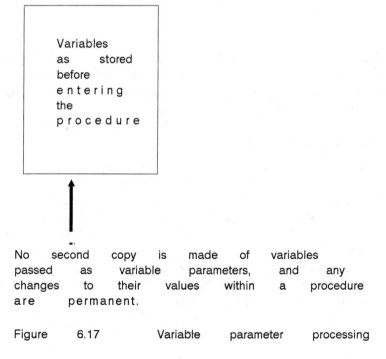

No second copy is made of variables passed as variable parameters, and any changes to their values within a procedure are permanent.

Figure   6.17   Variable   parameter   processing

Value Parameter	**Variable parameter**
Store the value of the variable on entry to the procedure.	Store the address of the variable on entry procedure.

Figure 6.18

C provides only value parameters, but we may learn the lesson from the way in which Pascal *actually operates* in order to *construct our own variable parameters*. To produce a function call using a value parameter, we simply pass the variable to the function. In order to produce the effect of a variable parameter, we must pass a pointer to the variable rather than the variable itself. This means that we are having to construct our own variable parameters, whereas Pascal would do it for us. On the other hand, provided we know what we are doing in C, the statements needed to use variable and value parameters are not intrinsically any more complex than their counterparts in Pascal (figure 6.19).

4) Files

C provides all the necessary tools to allow for file handling programs: fopen(), and fclose() allow for files to be opened and closed, while fputs(), fprintf(), and fgets(), fscanf(), allow data to be put into and read from files. Random access files can be created by using the fseek() function which allows for the file to be treated like an array and gives access to any item within the file.

These functions may be combined by the programmer to write file handling programs, but in practice it is often simpler to write a program using a commercial add-on library which supports a particular type of file processing- and which will itself use the basic file-handling commands. Hence, instead of the programmer being restricted to the rudimentary ascii files of text supported by the basic file handling facilities, listed above, much more complex files of records may be established and accessed, perhaps using indexed sequential processing with the help of an add-on library of file handling functions.

Who uses C?

There are three principal groups of people who program using C.

1) The writers of operating systems and systems software.

2) The writers of general applications.

3) The writers of specialised applications for interfacing.

All three groups benefit from the modular approach to programming offered by C, and the flexibility to design programs which operate in a specific way, and the power to tailor almost all the standard functions by developing specialised libraries. The applications programmers benefit particularly from the widespread availability of ready written add-on libraries. Interfacing problems can often be coded in C with the use of add-on libraries far more quickly than in other languages.

The relative portability of C programs provides an added incentive, since time spent developing a C application for a new environment is likely to be far less than for many competing languages. Although the current lack of any finalised and certified implementations of a rigorously defined standard causes some problems for programmers needing to write portable code. It has therefore been necessary to select particular C programming environments for the development of the programs in the next section. In order to reflect the two current C 'standards' in widespread use, each of the example programs has been tested using 'Zortech C version 2' which follows the Kernighan and Ritchie standard and 'Turbo C version 2.0' which follows the draft ANSI standard. In cases where the program differs between the two versions, details of the differences are given. The reader should note that although the versions of C in use here follow the two main standards, there can be minor differences when compared with other compilers which are also following the same standards. This is the immediate result of the lack of recognised conformance testing.

C Applications

In this chapter, perhaps more than any other, there is a difficulty in providing a series of examples which illustrate *typical* uses of C in areas where the language is strong. This is not because of shortcomings in the language, but rather because the language is flexible and powerful so that it can be used to good effect in almost any programming area. This combines with the widespread availability of add-on libraries to make nonsense of the claim that any single application is 'typical' for C. Additionally, because C is frequently used for the development of large-scale programs such as operating systems and commercial applications packages, many C programs are very much longer than space permits in this section. It is interesting to note that in Berry, Meekings and Soren (1988) the discussion of the major example program runs from page 117 to page 185, most of which is simply C source listing!

We shall therefore consider a number of examples which illustrate typical constructions using the C languge within the context of rather simple applications.

Example 1

For the first two example programs, we shall consider the claim that C allows programs to be written in a very economical way. With this in mind, figure 6.20 gives a C listing of a program which uses a 1-dimensional array of integers representing the number of days in each of the twelve months in the year. The program in figure 6.20 is written using conventional programming techniques and is typical of programs developed in other languages involving similar techniques.

Figure 6.21 is a second program which is equivalent to the one given in figure 6.20, but this time the features of C which allow for more compact source code and faster executing object code have been used. You will immediately detect the advantages of length in the latter listing. The question of whether the brevity sacrifices some of the clarity is a matter of personal judgement.

Notice how, in figure 6.21, the limit on the size of the array is provided by the computer counting for itself the number of entries contained in the initialising list. It is also important to appreciate that arrays in C are indexed from 0 and therefore the highest index in an array of size 12 is 11.

```
#include <stdio.h>
int mnthlngth[12];
main()
{
int month,daysinmonth;
initialise();
```

```
printf("Type in the number of the month\n");

scanf("%i",&month);

daysinmonth = mnthlngth[month-1];

printf("There are %i days in month number %i\n",day-
sinmonth,month);

}

initialise() /* The ANSI standard requires 'void in-
itialise(void)' */

{

extern int mnthlngth[];

mnthlngth[0] = 31;

mnthlngth[1] = 28;

mnthlngth[2] = 31;

mnthlngth[3] = 30;

mnthlngth[4] = 31;

mnthlngth[5] = 30;

mnthlngth[6] = 31;

mnthlngth[7] = 31;

mnthlngth[8] = 30;

mnthlngth[9] = 31;

mnthlngth[10] = 30;

mnthlngth[11] = 31;

}
```

Figure 6.20 The conventional programmer's attempt at month to day conversion.

```
#include <stdio.h>

int mnthlngth[] = {31,28,31,30,31,30,
31,31,30,31,30,31};

main()

{
```

```
int month,daysinmonth;
printf("Type in the number of the month\n");
scanf("%i",&month);
daysinmonth = mnthlngth[month-1];
printf("There are %i days in month number %i\n",day-
sinmonth,month);
}
```

Figure 6.21 A more compact version of figure 6.20.

Exercise 6.22 Following the examples above, try to write a program which stores the amount taken in a day by each of 20 checkout operators in a supermarket, and which will output the total takings for the day.

Note: If you wish to store the amounts of money as decimal values, then you will need to declare the type as 'float' rather than 'int'.

Example 2

As a second example which illustrates how C programs can be written very economically, the program which follows converts a series of sentences into code. The code method is to replace each character with the one immediately following it in the alphabet. Thus

```
Mary had a little lamb
```

becomes

```
Nbsz!ibe!b!mjuumf!mbnc
```

Notice that the spaces are replaced by an exclamation mark, since this is the character which follows <space> in the ASCII character set.

In order to provide a program which can cope with a series of sentences on separate lines, we must be careful to treat ends of lines sensibly. The simplest program to write would convert each end of line marker into the next character in the list of character codes, but this would not really be the most appropriate action to take. It would be more sensible to leave each end of line marker alone so that the encoded message remains in the original format. This is the approach adopted here.

The example is given in two forms. Figure 6.24 gives a more compact version of figure 6.23. Again, the reader is invited to consider how much loss of readability results from the more compact version.

Note. In order to run these programs, type in the message to be encoded a line at a time. The encoded message will be output for each line. To finish, type a # followed by RETURN.

```c
#include <stdio.h>
main()
{
  char ch;
  ch = getchar();
  /* read first character */
  while (ch != '#')
      {
      if (ch == '\n') putchar(ch);
      /* copy end of line markers */
          else { ch = ch + 1;
          /* encode all other characters */
      putchar(ch);
      }
  ch = getchar();
  /* read next character */
  }
printf(" End of message \n");
}
```

Figure 6.23 Encoding program

```
#include <stdio.h>
main()
{
char ch;
while ((ch = getchar()) != '#')
  {
  if (ch == '\n')
      putchar(ch);
      /* copy end of line markers */
  else
      {
      putchar(++ch); /* encode all others */
      }
  }
printf(" End of message \n");
}
```

Figure 6.24 Encoding program using more efficient programming style.

Exercise 6.25 Write a decoding program similar to the programs in figure 6.23 and 6.24.

Example 3

This third example has been chosen to be rather more representative of current programming practice for applications programmers who use the C language. The program uses an include file which provides an add-on library of functions which provide for windows to be produced on the computer's screen.

The library in use here is the **Shareware** package *'The Window BOSS'* by Phil. Mongelluzzo. This provides for the use of the following functions (among others):

wn_open which opens a window at a specified position,

wn_close(windowpointer) which closes a window,

wn_printf which works like printf, except output is in a specified window

v_getch() which behaves like getchar() but from within a window.

Figure 6.26 lists a program which uses these four functions in order to display a series of 3 windows on the screen. Figure 6.27 shows the appearance of the screen on running the program when the specified point is reached.

Note: The Window BOSS package used here has been tested with Turbo C. It is not advertised for use with Zortech C.

```c
#include <stdio.h>
#include <windows.h>
main()
{
WINDOWPTR w1;
WINDOWPTR w2;
WINDOWPTR w3;
int watrib;
int batrib;
batrib = v_setatr(BLUE,WHITE,0,0);
watrib = v_setatr(WHITE,BLACK,0,0); /* set colours */
w1 = wn_open(0,10,10,18,10,watrib,batrib);
wn_printf(w1,"Window 1 is open\n");
v_getch();
w2 = wn_open(0,10,10,8,5,watrib,batrib);
wn_printf(w2,"This\n is\nwindow 2\n"); /* Figure 6.27
shows screen at this point in program */
v_getch();
wn_close(w2);
```

```
wn_printf(w1,"Window 2 has gone\n");
v_getch();
w3 = wn_open(0,5,5,60,16,watrib,batrib);
wn_printf(w3,"Here is a big window\n");
v_getch();
wn_close(w3);
v_getch();
wn_close(w1);
}
```

Figure 6.26 A program which uses a standard window library.

Exercise 6.28 Find a current software catalogue and investigate the variety of C add-on libraries available for common operating systems. What implementations of C are most widely supported by the add-ons?

Example 4

Example 4 considers the low-level uses of C. The program uses the bitwise binary operarions to illustrate how some of these might be used.

For the reader accustomed to dealing with computer binary arithmetic, the use of SHIFT operators to multiply and divide by 2 will be familiar, as will the facilities of bitwise AND and OR operations. For the uninitiated, the following examples should be of assistance:

Take the number 43, for example, whose binary representation is (00101011). A single place shift to the left yields the binary number (01010110) which is 86 (multiplication by 2) while a shift to the right yields 00010101 which is 21 (division by 2 discarding the remainder).

The logical (bitwise) AND operation takes two binary numbers and produces an answer made up of a 1 in each place where both the original numbers had a 1 and a zero everywhere else.

Thus (00101011) AND (10101101) gives the answer (00101001)

The logical (bitwise) OR operation gives an answer made up of 1 in each place where either of the original number had a 1 and 0 only where both original numbers were zero.

Thus (00101011) OR (10101101) gives the answer (10101111)

These operations can be very useful in interfacing programs where a particular bit value within the input from a port may be significant, and inputs from different ports may be combined using ANDs and ORs to

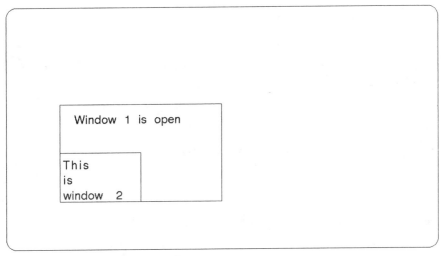

Figure 6.27

give a final value (as in a security system where we might be looking for a breach of EITHER a window OR a door).

The program listed in figure 6.29 takes in two integers from the keyboard. It examines the 4th bit (from the left) in the binary representation of the first number and the 7th bit in the binary representation of the second number. The computer bell is sounded if either of these bits is a 1.

```
#include <stdio.h>
main()
{
int num1,num2;
int mask1 = 16;
int mask2 = 2;
```

```
printf("Type in first number\n");
scanf("%i",&num1);
printf("Type in second number\n");
scanf("%i",&num2);
num1 = num1 & mask1; /* & is
logical bitwise AND */
num2 = num2 & mask2; /* | is logical bitwise OR */
num1 = num1 | num2 < 3; /* < is Left Shift operator */
if (num1 == 16)
  {
  printf("Beep");
  putchar('\007'); /* Bell character */
  }
}
```

Figure 6.29 A simple bit-manipulation program.

Exercise 6.30 Adapt the program given in figure 6.29 to accept two integers as input and sound the system bell if the first bit in the binary representation of the first number is a one and the eighth bit in the binary representation of the second number is also a 1.

C's Limitations

C is arguably the most adaptable of the languages discussed in this book, and it is hard to identify any particular application areas where it is weak. It is however important to take note of the fact that C is nevertheless not necessarily a good choice in all circumstances.

1) C is a dangerous language for the inexperienced: Unlike most modern high-level languages, C is tolerant of misuses of its facilities by the programmer. This has been identified as one of the great strengths of the language, since it does not impose its own method of doing things on the programmer, but leaves the programmer free to *break* the normal rules wherever necessary in order to write a good program. This strength turns into a weakness when used by an inexperienced programmer who

will not necessarily be warned by the compiler of the reason for some failure in a program.

2) C programs may be difficult to debug: The C programmer has freedom to develop his programs in his own way. The language permits for very economical expression of the language statements within a program, and if this is coupled with poor documentation, the programmer presented with another programmer's work may be faced with a harder task than would be the case with some languages. This is not really a direct criticism of the C language, but rather of the way in which it is used by some programmers. It is a sad fact that the economy of expression offered by the language can make life more difficult later.

3) Standardisation: The lack of standardisation and the inevitable variations between implementations of a language which offers low-level facilities is a problem which, it may be hoped, will disappear as the ANSI standard specification becomes accepted.

4) Highly specialised applications: where a specialist language exists for a particular application area it is frequently more efficient to program in the specialist language than in C, despite the flexibility afforded by C. The question which must be addressed is 'Would an experienced C programmer write a better program in C than in the specialist language for this application?' The answer to this question will depend on such issues as: the type of problem, the appropriateness of any add-on libraries available in C, the difficulty of learning the alternative language, and the portability required in the solution.

7 Modula-2

Introduction

This chapter is concerned with the programming language Modula-2. Modula-2 is the most recent of all the languages discussed here and, as a consequence, displays many features which are consistent with the more modern approaches to computer programming.

Background

Modula-2 has its roots in Pascal. Niklaus Wirth, the originator of the Pascal language had designed Pascal to be particularly suited to the teaching of programming. For the reasons which we discussed earlier, Pascal has become much more widely used than Wirth had intended, and as a result of this, a number of shortcomings in the language came to light.

Many implementors of Pascal sought to close the gaps in the language by designing Pascal versions with particular extensions, and this brought about a loss in the *portability* of programs. Standardisation had been one of the design goals of the original language.

Wirth was faced with the problem of having designed a very well accepted language, but one which was becoming less and less standardised, and also was becoming progressively less appropriate as the technology advanced well beyond its state when Pascal had been designed.

Rather than design a new standard for an extended Pascal, which might, in any case, fail to attract widespread acceptance among the implementors, Wirth set about designing a new language, which would be a successor to Pascal, preserving the main features which made Pascal accepted, but also building in features which had been missed out of the original Pascal specification, either because they had been inappropriate to the technology of that time, or because they were not required of a language designed purely as a teaching language.

Wirth used his ideas to develop the experimental language Modula in 1975. With the experiences of people using Modula, Modula-2 was designed and released in 1979. In essence, Modula-2 was an enhanced version of Modula.

The design of Modula-2 was motivated from the desire to develop a successor to Pascal, but to describe the language merely in those terms is to do Wirth an injustice, since Modula-2 marks the beginning of a new approach to programming. It reflects the more highly structured approaches being developed to the writing of computer programs in the late 1970's. Wirth defines a new approach to problem solving: modularity. Modularity refers to the breaking down of each section of a problem into a series of sub-problems or modules. These modules may then be developed in isolation in the Modula-2 language, and combined later in order to produce the whole program.

Modularity can be seen as a natural extension of the previous use of procedures in Pascal, which also provided for this structured design and development of the program but without allowing for quite the same degree of independence. However, the use of modules can, as we shall see later, result in the easy development of library modules which can be incorporated into many programs. This approach is very similar to the use of library facilities in languages such as C. However, we shall find that the use of modules in Modula-2 is very much easier for the programmer than corresponding constructions in other languages. This is mainly because Wirth, in designing Modula-2 in the late 1970's, was able to benefit from experiences of users of a variety of other languages, including C, in making the new specification. The advantages of Modula-2 are aptly summed up by Knepley and Platt (1985) 'Modula-2 combines the best features of Ada and C without their drawbacks'.

In addition to the fundamental design strategy introduced in Modula-2 (that is, the use of modules), there are two aspects of the language which are crucial to its acceptance as an applications programming language, particularly in the advanced climate provided by computers in the 1990's:

1) Modula-2 supports low level programming. It is therefore possible to address the hardware of the underlying computer system and improve the versatility of the programs being developed compared with traditional high-level languages. As a strongly typed language, Modula-2 might be expected to impose restrictions on low level work which would be undesirable. However, it is possible to discard some of the type checking in order to overcome this potential problem.

2) Modula-2 supports concurrency. Concurrency refers to the facility for the computer to be performing simultaneously more than one task. So, for example, we might find that an application would benefit from performing calculations while awatiing a user input at a keyboard. This would involve having the processor simultaneously running two pieces of program, one to process inputs at the keyboard and the other to perform the calculations. Most computer languages do not provide built-in facilities which make this possible, but Modula-2 does.

One might, with some justification, question how frequently the average programmer will need to use this concurrency. But in fact, with the design of the more up-to-date operating systems in use in the late 1980's on more sophisticated hardware installations, concurrency is becoming increasingly common. Indeed, the support of concurrency by the rival language ADA is one reason for its adoption for some scientific applications.

The official definition of the Modula-2 language was contained in Wirth (1982). Up to now, this document has been followed fairly closely by the implementors of Modula-2 compilers and therefore programs developed in Modula-2 are more portable than those written in many languages. However, there is not at this time any formal international standard for the language.

So Modula-2 has grown out of Pascal. It retains the good features of the Pascal language which we identified in chapter 3: Modula-2 is well suited to structured programming methods, it is a strongly typed language, and it is easy to implement in its 'standard' form. As we shall discover in the pages which follow, the programs which we described using Pascal can be transported to the Modula-2 environment with only very minor changes, and we meet an additional series of examples which build on the modularity of the language to provide more sophisticated programs more easily.

The first example program (figure 7.1a) gives a simple Modula-2 program which adds together two numbers and writes their sum on the computer screen. The Pascal version of this program is given for comparison in figure 7.1b.

```
MODULE Fig7point1a;
FROM IO IMPORT WrLn, WrStr, WrInt, RdInt;
VAR
firstno,secondno,sum : INTEGER;
ch : CHAR;
BEGIN
WrStr('Type in first number');
firstno:=RdInt();
WrStr('Type in second number');
secondno:=RdInt();
sum := firstno + secondno;
WrStr('The total of those two numbers is ');
WrInt(sum,5);
WrLn;
END Fig7point1a.
```

Figure 7.1a Modula-2 program which adds two integers and outputs the sum.

```
program fig7point1b(input,output);
var
firstno,secondno,sum : integer;
ch : char;
begin
```

```
writeln('Type in first number');
readln(firstno);
writeln('Type in second number');
readln(secondno);
sum := firstno + secondno;
writeln('The total of those two numbers is ',sum)
end.
```

Figure 7.1b Pascal version of the Modula-2 program in figure 7.1a.

We may observe immediately the close correspondence between the two programs listed in the figures above. There is an almost exact correspondence between the Pascal statements on the one hand, and the Modula-2 statements on the other. The one exception to this general rule is the IMPORT statement in the Modula-2 program. Modula-2 has no inbuilt input/output routines, but as in the C language, these are provided as an add-on facility by the language's implementors. The input and output procedures which we require here have been IMPORTED from this standard I/O library, which is known as IO. The precise names of the I/O libraries, and the procedures which they contain, may vary from one implementation of Modula-2 to another, but the facilities which we have used here are fairly typical. Separate procedures are provided for the input and output of different types of data. Thus WrInt is used to write an integer value, while WrStr is used to write out a string.

WrLn in Modula-2 outputs an end-of-line marker as does Writeln in Pascal, however the two procedures are not identical, since the Modula-2 WrLn only outputs an end-of-line, and so it must be preceded by separate statements which output any data required before the end of the current line. To illustrate this difference, consider the Pascal statement

```
writeln('Hello');
```

which outputs the word Hello followed by an end of line marker. In Modula-2 the corresponding code would be

```
WrStr('Hello');
WrLn;
```

Notice how the program name is preceded by the word MODULE. It is crucial in most Modula-2 implementations that the same name is given to a module internally (i.e. after the word 'MODULE') as it has externally (i.e. the name of the file in which it is stored in the computer system.) Thus, the program MODULE Fred would typically be stored on an MSDOS system using the filename FRED.MOD. Failure to observe this simple rule, which does not apply in most other languages, is a common cause of errors at compile time for the beginner to Modula-2 programming.

Modula-2's facilities

In this section, we shall turn our attention to the specific facilities offered by Modula-2. Naturally, it follows from the discussion earlier in the chapter that we shall often be able to describe the facilities simply by referring to the Pascal language. Most of the items which will be particularly interesting in the discussion will be those differences from Pascal which make the Modula-2 language particularly versatile.

Data types available in Modula-2 are broadly comparable to those offered to the Pascal programmer. The types INTEGER, BOOLEAN, REAL and CHAR are joined by types CARDINAL (positive integers with a larger maximum value than INTEGER allows) and STRING (although STRING is provided by library routines rather than being intrinsic to the standard language). All the usual facilities are offered to manipulate these data types. Sets and enumerated types are also available and behave similarly to their Pascal counterparts, as do arrays and records.

In the languages which we have met hitherto, looping constructions have fallen into two main classes. The count-controlled loop and the condition controlled loop. Modula-2 supports the FOR..DO..END construction which provides a count-controlled loop. This is illustrated in the example in figure 7.2.

```
MODULE Fig7point2;
FROM IO IMPORT WrInt, WrStr, WrLn;
VAR sum, i : INTEGER;
BEGIN
sum := 0;
FOR i := 1 TO 10 DO
  WrInt(i,3);
```

```
WrLn;
 sum := sum + i
END;
WrLn;
WrStr('Their total is ');
WrInt(sum,3);
WrLn
END Fig7point2.
```

Figure 7.2

Condition-controlled loops typically fall into two classes, those which check the condition on entry, and those which check the condition at the end. Modula-2 adds a third type of exit condition checking, which allows the programmer to choose any point (or points) within the body of the loop and to check and exit at that point. The three condition-controlled looping constructions in Modula-2 are:

```
REPEAT...UNTIL...
```

which has checking at the end of the loop

```
WHILE...DO...END
```

which provides checking at the beginning of the loop

and

```
LOOP...EXIT...END
```

which provides checking at any point.

Naturally, it would have been possible for the language to have offered only the LOOP...EXIT...END construction, since it allows the use of checking anywhere, including the beginning and the end, but REPEAT and WHILE constructions are now sufficiently familiar to most programmers as to make their inclusion highly desirable in any computer language. Figure 7.3, 7.4 and 7.5 illustrate typical uses of the three types of condition-controlled loop. Notice how much more easily the program in figure 7.6 is to write using the LOOP...EXIT...END construction, than the corresponding Pascal version in figure 7.7 which is naturally unable to use this technique.

```
MODULE Fig7point3;
FROM IO IMPORT WrStr, RdInt, WrInt, WrLn;
VAR sum, i : INTEGER;
BEGIN
WrStr('Type  in  a  list  of  integers,  terminated  by
zero.');
WrLn;
sum := 0;
REPEAT
    WrStr('Next number');
    WrLn;
    i := RdInt();
    sum := sum + i
UNTIL i = 0;
WrStr('The total of those numbers is ');
WrInt(sum,5);
END Fig7point3.
```

Figure 7.3

```
MODULE Fig7point4;
FROM IO IMPORT RdInt, WrLn, WrStr, WrInt;
VAR x, sum : INTEGER;
BEGIN
WrStr('Type in initial sum deposited');
WrLn;
x := RdInt();
sum := x;
WHILE sum < 1000 DO
```

```
    WrStr('Not enough money yet');
    WrLn;
    WrStr('How much more are you depositing?');
    WrLn;
    x := RdInt();
    sum := sum + x
  END;
  WrStr('You now have enough money to buy your holi-
day');
  WrLn
END Fig7point4.
```

Figure 7.4

```
MODULE Fig7point5;
FROM IO IMPORT WrStr, WrLn, WrInt, RdInt;
VAR x, sum : INTEGER;
BEGIN
WrStr('Type in a list of positive integers, ended
with a negative integer');
  WrLn;
  sum := 0;
  LOOP
    WrStr('Next number');
    WrLn;
    x := RdInt();
    IF x < 0 THEN EXIT END;
    sum := sum + x
  END;
  WrStr('The total of those numbers, excluding the
negative one, was ');
```

```
WrInt(sum,5);
WrLn
END Fig7point5.
```

Figure 7.5

```
MODULE Fig7point6;
FROM IO IMPORT RdChar, WrStr, WrLn;
VAR Choice : CHAR;
PROCEDURE English;
BEGIN
WrStr('This is the English procedure');
WrLn
END English;
PROCEDURE Mathematics;
BEGIN
WrStr('This is the Mathematics procedure');
WrLn
END Mathematics;
PROCEDURE History;
BEGIN
WrStr('This is the History procedure');
WrLn
END History;
BEGIN
WrStr('Type in your choice of subject');
WrLn;
WrStr('1. English');
WrLn;
WrStr('2. Mathematics');
```

```
WrLn;
WrStr ('3. History');
WrLn;
LOOP
    Choice := RdChar ();
    CASE Choice OF
      '1': English; EXIT|
      '2': Mathematics; EXIT|
      '3': History; EXIT ;
    END
END
END Fig7point6.
```

Figure 7.6

```
program menu (input, output);
var choice:char;
procedure english;
begin
writeln('This is the English procedure')
end;
procedure mathematics;
begin
writeln('This is the Mathematics procedure')
end;
procedure history;
begin
writeln('This is the History procedure')
end;
begin
```

```
writeln('Please enter your choice of subject');
writeln('1. English');
writeln('2. Mathematics');
writeln('3. History');
repeat
    readln(choice)
until choice in ['1','2','3'];
case choice of
    '1' : english;
    '2' : mathematics;
    '3' : history
end
end.
```

Figure 7.7 A Pascal version of program in figure 7.6 which replaces the LOOP statement with a repeat loop.

Decisions in Modula-2 follow the Pascal pattern very closely. Two constructions, IF and CASE are provided, and these give the flexibility to program most constructions normally required.

Recursion is supported in a way which corresponds to Pascal.

One of the strengths of Pascal which we identified was the ability to allocate data storage as a program executes using so-called dynamic variables. We may recall that the strong typing of the Pascal language insists that all data types are declared at the beginning of the program, procedure or function, and the variables allocated then are static, that is, their positions in the memory are identified and the memory used is allocated at the start. These static data contrast with dynamic data, whose location is determined when the NEW procedure is encountered. Modula-2 supports dynamic data in a similar way to Pascal, by providing the procedures NEW and DISPOSE which work just as their Pascal counterparts. However, Modula-2 also uses a module usually called 'Storage' which provides two additional procedures: ALLOCATE and DEALLOCATE. The ALLOCATE procedure is used by NEW to allocate the necessary areas of the computer's memory for the storage of the data referred to in the NEW statement. Similarly, DEALLOCATE is used by DISPOSE to recover the used memory locations which are no longer required.

There are benefits in the way in which NEW and DISPOSE are implemented in terms of the ALLOCATE and DEALLOCATE procedures. Firstly, it is possible for NEW and DISPOSE to be defined in a machine independent way, because the machine dependence of the method of actually choosing and allocating the memory to a data item is performed by the add-on facility in the Storage module. This in turn helps the implementors of the language. However, for the programmer there is also an advantage, because the procedures ALLOCATE and DEALLOCATE are available to the individual programmer as well as the procedures NEW and DISPOSE. Hence the programmer can have more control over the way in which memory is allocated and recovered if he chooses to use it. This reflects Modula-2's suitability for the development of programs at low level.

The major advance in computer language design which is reflected in the way Modula-2 is used is in the preparation by the programmer of modules which may be prepared completely independently and compiled separately for later linkage into the completed program. This is a clear benefit to the team of programmers who may work separately on parts of a problem and then combine the separate sections at a later stage when each has been fully and independently tested. It can also be very advantageous to those who write several similar computer programs and would need to use similar techniques to produce each program. The construction of library modules containing generic procedures which may then be incorporated in many programs is very attractive.

Unfortunately, there is a significant problem which can arise in designing these generic procedures, particularly when arrays need to be passed as parameters. Imagine, for example the situation when we wish to produce a procedure which will take a 1-dimensional array of integers and return the array after each element has been multiplied by 2.

In this situation, we desire a procedure which will take the array

```
1 2 3 4 5 6
```

and produce as output

```
2 4 6 8 10 12
```

However, it would be useful if the procedure could also take the array

```
1 2  3  4
```

which is a different 'shape' and produce the corresponding output

```
2  4  6  8
```

In Pascal, this would not have been possible before the adoption of the latest standard, because we would have been forced to define the array type in the procedure definition. This array type would then restrict the size of the array which could be applied as parameter. There were one or two rather fiddly ways of overcoming the problem using Pascal, by making every array the same size by the insertion of zeroes as necessary. This was clearly only partly satisfactory, and Modula-2 provides an alternative strategy through the use of the 'open array parameter'. The current Pascal standard offers *conformant array parameters*, which behave similarly.

When we write a procedure which uses open array parameters, we are warning the compiler that the variable passed to the procedure will be an array, but that the actual dimensions of the array will only be determined later.

The program in figure 7.8 illustrates the use of open array parameters.

```
MODULE Fig7point8;

FROM IO IMPORT RdInt, WrStr, WrInt, WrLn;

VAR a : ARRAY [0..9] OF INTEGER;

b : ARRAY [0..19] OF INTEGER;

Tot1, Tot2, j : INTEGER;

PROCEDURE Addup(x:ARRAY OF INTEGER):INTEGER;

VAR i, Subtot : INTEGER;

BEGIN

Subtot := 0;

FOR i := 0 TO HIGH(x) DO

    Subtot := Subtot + x[i]

END;
```

```
RETURN Subtot
END Addup;
BEGIN
WrStr('Type in ten integers');
WrLn;
FOR j := 0 TO 9 DO
    a[j] := RdInt()
END;
Tot1 := Addup(a);
WrStr('Now type in twenty integers');
WrLn;
FOR j := 0 TO 19 DO
    b[j] := RdInt()
END;
Tot2 := Addup(b);
WrStr('The totals are, respectively, ');
WrInt(Tot1,4);
WrStr(' and ');
WrInt(Tot2,4);
WrLn
END Fig7point8.
```

Figure 7.8

This program takes two arrays of integers, the first containing 10 integers, and the second containing 20 integers, and uses, in each case, the procedure Addup to calculate the total of all the entries in the array. These Open Array Parameters are just one of the ways in which the strong-typing of Modula-2 can be relaxed when the programmer need extra flexibility.

Exercise 7.9 The program in figure 7.8 has two separate loops to allow the input of the two arrays of different sizes. Write a program which uses a procedure with open array parameters to replace this repeated code.

Modula-2 has two different types of procedure. The PROCEDURE corresponds to the procedure in Pascal, while the FUNCTION PRO-CEDURE corrsponds to Pascal's function, and accordingly returns a value of the type specified in the FUNCTION PROCEDURE's declaration.

Separate Compilation

One of the features of Modula-2 which we have already identified as being important in the development of programs is the facility to write separate modules containing code which may be compiled independently. It is the independent compilation rather than the separate development of the modules which is particularly significant, since it introduces a rather interesting problem:

How can a language such as Modula-2, which is strongly typed and has the rigorous error checking built in which this strong typing implies, make use of procedures within one module which are defined elsewhere?

We came across the independent development of sections of program when we discussed the C language, which again permitted the separate compilation and linking of different sections of object code, but C was a rather different type of language from Modula-2. C is a language which tolerates mismatches of types, and which allows the programmer to gain additional flexibility by 'breaking' rules. For the C programmer who wants strict checking, a separate program *LINT* is often supplied which performs this. Modula-2 on the other hand, aims to prevent this type of rule breaking and impose a much more rigid discipline on the program-mer. In order to maintain consistency and error checking it is not possible to have completely independent compilation of separate modules in Modula-2, since the compiler does at least require some statement about the specifications of those objects which are defined in other modules, even if the detail of the module's implementation are not available to it.

This apparent contradiction between, on the one hand, the need to have other modules available when compiling an individual module and, on the other hand, the desire to have modules compiled independently, is overcome by the existence of three different types of module developed when programming an application in Modula-2. These are the 'program module', the 'definition module', and the 'implementation module'.

The program module contains the main program. In general this module will call upon procedures which are described in other modules. For each such module there will be a definition module and an implementation module.

The definition module describes in outline what a particular module contains. It states for example what procedures from library and other modules will be required in order to compile the module, and it also describes the procedures within the present module, in terms of the types of parameters which they require, and the types of any values which are returned. The definition module does not, however, make any attempt to describe how the procedures are implemented. An example of a definition module is given in figure 7.10.

```
DEFINITION MODULE Demo;

EXPORT QUALIFIED

Readinnum;

FROM IO IMPORT WrStr, WrLn, RdInt;

PROCEDURE Readinnum(VAR X : INTEGER);

END Demo.
```

Figure 7.10 A simple definition module

Notice in this example how there is an **EXPORT** list as well as an **IMPORT** list. The EXPORT list gives details of the objects which are defined within the module which will become available outside it. (That is, those objects which may be used by other modules.) The word **QUALIFIED** in the EXPORT statement describes how the compiler is to deal with any possible occurence of clashes between object identifiers within different modules. The procedures defined within the module Demo will need to be IMPORTED explicitly by other modules, or else will be described using a Qualified identifier, thus: Demo.Readinnum (see figures 7.12 and 7.13 below).

The definition module does not contain any details of the way in which the procedures are to be executed. This is the purpose of the implementation module which is developed separately. The implementation module contains details of how the procedures in a particular module are to be implemented. It is the implementation module which describes the sequence of instructions which are to be performed in completing each procedure within the module. (See figure 7.11).

```
IMPLEMENTATION MODULE Demo;

FROM IO IMPORT WrStr, WrLn, RdInt;

PROCEDURE Readinnum(VAR X:INTEGER);

BEGIN

WrStr('Type in the value of an integer');

WrLn;

X := RdInt()

END

END Demo
```

Figure 7.11 An implementation module corresponding to the definition module given in fugure 7.10.

If we now consider again the problem of separate compilation of modules, we may observe that, provided that the definition modules of all the other modules are available at compile time, the compiler will have all the information necessary to perform the error checking. It will have no need to use any implementation modules except for that being currently compiled. We may therefore develop the implementation of each module entirely independently so long as the definition of each module is pre-determined.

At first glance, the requirement to pre-define the definition modules might seem rather restrictive, but on further consideration it becomes evident that it is not only acceptable but indeed a necessary requirement in any team of independent people developing software, since the definition modules simply list a subset of the specification details which must certainly be agreed before any programming is begun. In a large programming team, the chief programmer could be responsible for producing all the definition modules before any of the individual programmers started work.

Having introduced the concept of definition and implementation modules, we shall consider how their contents may be used. The fundamental idea relates to the development of a library of modules which contain useful procedures, and these modules supplement the library modules which are supplied with the Modula-2 implementation. The programmer has the choice of IMPORTING either a list of explicit procedures from the library modules available, or to IMPORT the entire contents of one or more modules.

Figure 7.12 illustrates how specific procedures are imported from a library module, and figure 7.13 indicates the alternative of importing a whole module. Notice how the references to individual procedures imported do not need to give their library module name as a qualifier, whereas those procedures imported as a whole module must be addressed by their module name.

```
MODULE Importspecificprocedures;

FROM IO IMPORT WrStr, WrLn;

BEGIN

WrStr('We may refer to specific procedures by their
shortened names');

WrLn

END

END Importspecificprocedures.
```

Figure 7.12

```
MODULE Importthewholelibrary;

IMPORT IO;

BEGIN

IO.WrStr('This time we need to qualify the name of
each procedure imported by its library module name');

IO.WrLn

END;

END Importthewholelibrary.
```

Figure 7.13

Concurrency

In most conventional programming situations, we define the processes which the computer is to undertake as a sequence of operations, which will be performed in the order listed. The computer processor is then assumed to dedicate its resources to the single program.

For many years, large mainframe computers have allowed multitasking or multiprogramming. This refers simply to the notion of using a single processor in which more than one task or program is currently active. Typically this has referred to a situation where users of different terminals have each been able to have a job active within the large computer at the same time, and have each received their share of processor time and power.

Desktop computers have become increasingly powerful, so that they too may have significantly under-utilised processor power, but sharing of the processor by several users is not usually economic. On the other hand, it is becoming common to identify different tasks which a single user might need which may be undertaken concurrently by the processor.

Modula-2 is one of very few programming languages which has reacted to the demand for concurrent processing of tasks, and the facilities which are provided by the language require some thought.

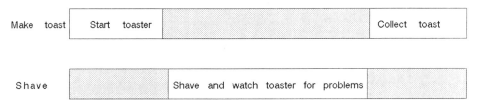

Figure 7.14 The activities of making toast and shaving can be performed concurrently

Figure 7.14 illustrates how I might use the time taken to toast two slices of bread in the morning to shave. This demands that I can leave the toaster to get on with its job while it does not need any of my attention, and I can turn my attention to shaving. However, I am ready to react to the toaster (and stop shaving) if something should go wrong.

We may draw some elementary conclusions from this simple example:

1) There are periods of time when the toaster does not require my attention and I would be otherwise idle.

2) When I am shaving, the toaster can interrupt me if it needs

attention

3) The two tasks of shaving and making toast do not interdepend, and I can save time by multi-tasking in this way.

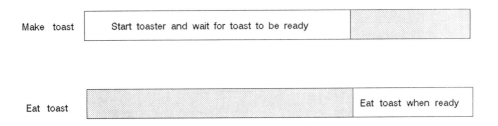

Figure 7.15   Making toast and eating toast cannot be performed concurrently

Now consider the two tasks of making toast and eating toast (figure 7.15). It is clear that no multi-tasking solution to this problem will speed things up (at least not unless I want four slices and make two more while eating the first two!)

When defining tasks which are to be performed concurrently we need to follow this same practice. We need to make certain that neither task needs output or results from the other, and it is also worth checking that the processor does indeed have some spare capacity while performing each task in order to avoid the situation where time is actually lost because of the processor activity involved to cope with the concurrent processes.

Figure 7.16 shows the practicalities of setting up 'coprocesses' to run concurrently. The TRANSFER instruction is used to transfer the processing from one coroutine to another.

```
MODULE Concurrentprocess;

VAR ProcessA, ProcessB, Main : ADDRESS;

PROCEDURE A;

BEGIN

{definition of Procedure A which should include the
instruction 'TRANSFER(ProcessA,ProcessB)' at the point
```

```
of transfer to the other procedure}

    END A;

    PROCEDURE B;

    BEGIN

    {definition of Procedure B which should include the
instruction 'TRANSFER(ProcessB,ProcessA)' at the point
of transfer to the other procedure}

    END B;

    BEGIN

    NEWPROCESS(A,ADR(A),SIZE(A),ProcessA);

    NEWPROCESS(B,ADR(B),SIZE(B),ProcessB);

    TRANSFER(Main,ProcessA)

    END Concurrent process.
```

Figure 7.16

Notice how the position in each procedure must be determined where transfer of processing to the other procedure must happen. Transfer will return to the main program when the end of the two concurrent procedures is reached.

The procedure NEWPROCESS requires details of the procedure to be introduced as a process, its address and workspace size and the reference name for the process within the program. The address and workspace size are available through the use of the built-in functions ADR() and SIZE(). The reference name is necessary in case the same procedure is called (perhaps with different parameters) as more than one of the concurrent processes.

Exercise 7.17 Try to think of some processes which would lend themselves to concurrency. You will probably be able to think of several from everyday life, but may find it harder to think of good computer programming examples.

Who uses Modula-2?

Modula-2 is not commonly used at present. It takes a considerable amount of time for a 'new' language to become widely accepted, and Modula-2 should still be considered new.

The main potential for Modula-2's acceptance is probably firstly as a teaching language which supercedes Pascal (or forms a natural second language after a course on Pascal) which also has the functionality of C without the disadvantages of C's less rigid rules of presentation. If it can gain acceptance in this area then its long-term success is assured.

On the other hand, it is clear that there are already at least five leading languages in different parts of the serious software development business. These are:

COBOL in business file processing

C in applications development

Pascal in the learning environment

FORTRAN and ADA in scientific applications.

Modula-2 has the flexibility and functionality to perform well in any or all of these situations, and it is this flexibility which is its particular strength. Its weakness is that there is probably no particular reason to motivate change among users from their accustomed language (after all, this is how we accounted earlier for the continued strength of FORTRAN and COBOL use). Only time will tell whether Modula-2 gains widespread acceptance, but it is likely to become the first choice programming language for Computer Science students..

Modula-2 Applications

We have identified already the similarity of Modula-2 to Pascal, and it would be fruitless to re-present the examples from Pascal in Modula-2 although it would be very easy to do this. This is left as an exercise to the reader, and instead we shall look here at two example programs which benefit from the concurrency offered by the language, and which would be difficult to implement in most high level languages and a further example which benefits greatly from the use of a library module.

Example 1.

In this first example we shall apply Modula-2's interrupt handling ability (that is, the ability to await action within one process while continuing to execute a different process) to run two procedures concurrently. Typical applications of this type of program occur when processing of a continuous calculation is interrupted for data input by another process. Most high level languages would require specialised low level programming incorporated within the high level program in order to give access to these interrupts.

In order to keep the procedures simple, we shall have the computer continuously counting from 1 to 1000 and restarting at 1 in the one process, while awaiting input of a list of 10 integers to be summed as the other process. Naturally, if the second process is run in isolation, a significant proportion of the processor's time is spent in awaiting a user-input, and this is the time which can be allocated to the first process.

This program (listed in figure 7.18) uses the procedure KeyPressed() to detect when a key has been pressed to input one of the numbers, and at that point returns control from the Counting process to the Total process. You may observe that the counting is suspended until the number has been typed in and the Return key has been pressed.

```
MODULE Fig7point18;
FROM IO IMPORT WrStr, WrInt, WrLn, RdInt, KeyPressed;
FROM Window IMPORT GotoXY;
FROM SYSTEM IMPORT NEWPROCESS, TRANSFER, ADDRESS;
CONST WspSze = 1000;
VAR Main, Proc1, Proc2 : ADDRESS;
WkSpce1,WkSpce2:ARRAY[1..WspSze] OF BYTE;
PROCEDURE Counting;
VAR X : INTEGER;
BEGIN
REPEAT
    FOR X:=1 TO 1000 DO
      GotoXY(5,5);
      WrInt(X,5);
      IF KeyPressed() THEN TRANSFER(Proc2,Proc1) END
    END
UNTIL FALSE
END Counting;
```

```
PROCEDURE Total;
VAR I, Sum, X : INTEGER;
BEGIN
Sum := 0;
FOR I := 1 TO 10 DO
    GotoXY(10,20);
    WrStr('Type in your next number ');
    GotoXY(36,20);
    WrInt(I,1);
    WrStr(' ');
    TRANSFER(Proc1,Proc2);
    GotoXY(38,20);
    X:=RdInt();
    Sum := Sum + X
END;
WrLn;
WrStr('The total was ');
WrInt(Sum,6);
WrLn;
TRANSFER(Proc1,Main)
END Total;
BEGIN
NEWPROCESS(Total,ADR(WkSpce1),1000,Proc1);
NEWPROCESS(Counting,ADR(WkSpce2),1000,Proc2);
TRANSFER(Main,Proc1)
END Fig7point18.
```

Figure 7.18.

Example 2

The program in figure 7.19 illustrates an alternative approach to solving the problem from example 1, this time using a time-slicing facility provided in one of the Library Modules within the TopSpeed Modula-2 system.

Time slicing has the advantage that the Counting procedure is not interrupted for the whole time taken to type in each integer, but has the disadvantage that time-slices are sometimes allocated to the Total procedure, even when there is no input to process.

In this program, the procedures Lock and Unlock are used to prevent the Scheduler interrupting execution in the middle of critical operations.

```
MODULE Fig7point19;

FROM IO IMPORT WrStr, WrInt, WrLn, RdInt;

FROM Window IMPORT GotoXY;

FROM Process IMPORT StartScheduler, StopScheduler,
StartProcess, Lock, Unlock;

PROCEDURE Counting;

VAR X : INTEGER;

BEGIN

REPEAT

FOR X:=1 TO 1000 DO

    Lock;

    GotoXY(5,5);

    WrInt(X,5);

    GotoXY(38,20);

    Unlock;

END

UNTIL FALSE

END Counting;

PROCEDURE Total;

VAR I, Sum, X : INTEGER;
```

```
BEGIN
Sum := 0;
FOR I := 1 TO 10 DO
    Lock;
    GotoXY(10,20);
    WrStr('Type in your next number ');
    GotoXY(36,20);
    WrInt(I,1);
    WrStr(' ');
    Unlock;
    X:=RdInt();
    Sum := Sum + X
END;
Lock;
WrLn;
WrStr('The total was ');
WrInt(Sum,6);
WrLn;
Unlock
END Total;
BEGIN
StartScheduler;
StartProcess(Counting,2000,1);
Total;
END Fig7point19.
```

Figure 7.19

Example 3

Modula-2 implementors provide a wide range of library procedures. Among them, typically, are various procedures to sort lists of data. Figure 7.20 illustrates the use of the QSort procedure from the TopSpeed Modula-2 library to perform a QuickSort on a list of 100 positive integers inputted at the keyboard.

```
MODULE Fig7point20;
FROM Lib IMPORT QSort;
FROM IO IMPORT RdInt, WrInt, WrStr, WrLn;
TYPE
List = ARRAY[1..100] OF CARDINAL;
VAR A:List;
PROCEDURE ReadList(VAR X:List);
VAR I:CARDINAL;
BEGIN
WrStr('Type in a list of 100 positive integers');
WrLn;
FOR I:=1 TO 100 DO
    WrStr('Number ');
    WrInt(I,3);
    WrStr(' ');
    X[I]:=RdInt();
    WrLn
END
END ReadList;
PROCEDURE WriteList(X:List);
VAR I : CARDINAL;
BEGIN
FOR I:=1 TO 100 DO
```

```
        WrInt(X[I],3);
        WrStr(' ')
END
END WriteList;
PROCEDURE Swap(I1,I2:CARDINAL);
VAR Tmp:CARDINAL;
BEGIN
Tmp:=A[I1];
A[I1]:=A[I2];
A[I2]:=Tmp
END Swap;
PROCEDURE Less(I1,I2:CARDINAL) : BOOLEAN;
BEGIN
RETURN A[I1] < A[I2]
END Less;
BEGIN
WrStr('Input the 100 numbers');
WrLn;
ReadList(A);
WrLn;
WrStr('Sort the 100 numbers');
QSort(100, Less, Swap);
WrLn;
WrStr('Here is the sorted list');
WrLn;
WriteList(A)
END Fig7point20.
```

Figure 7.20.

Modula-2's Limitations

We have remarked already on the high level of versatility of the Modula-2 language. From a functionality point of view, it has few limitations, except for the lack of standards and the relatively small number of experienced users of the language. This is reflected in the relatively small number of add-on libraries currently available. As compared with the C language, it is rather more likely that the Modula-2 programmer will need to develop his own 'standard' library modules.

From a programmer's viewpoint Modula-2 has many advantages over earlier languages, but some disadvantages too. In the Pascal chapter, we showed how much simpler really straightforward programs were to code using BASIC rather than Pascal. Modula-2 code is even more tedious to use for these very simple program than Pascal. Consider, for example the Pascal statement:

```
writeln('The answer when ',a,' is added to ',b,' is
',c);
```

In Modula-2 this would become:

```
WrStr('The answer when ');
WrInt(a);
WrStr(' is added to ');
WrInt(b);
WrStr(' is ');
WrInt(c);
WrLn;
```

While this is not an insurmountable problem, it could be argued that the complexity of this list of instructions would be unacceptable for a beginner, and that therefore it would be desirable to have experience in limited use of Pascal or some other language before attempting to use Modula-2.

8 Prolog

Introduction

In this chapter, we shall discuss the programming language Prolog, which is very different from the other languages which we have met. The techniques required of the programmer working in Prolog bear little resemblance to those used by programmers working in more traditional languages.

Background

The first official version of the Prolog language was developed by Alain Colmerauer at the University of Marseilles in the early 1970's. The intention was to provide an efficient language for programming in logic- and hence the name of the language: PRO-LOG. Early users of the language were almost exclusively academics and others engaged in specialist research, and it is comparatively recently (certainly within the mid- to late nineteen eighties) that Prolog has become commonly used by non-specialists. Today the language forms the basis for much of the developmental work in the field of artificial intelligence, and in the provision of expert systems.

Prolog may be categorised as a declarative language. This sets it apart from the other programming languages which we have met, all of which are referred to as procedural or algorithmic languages. The distinction between these two broad classes of language may perhaps best be understood by considering the role of the programmer in the development of software.

It is natural to think of the programmer as being presented with a particular problem which needs to be solved. There will be a number of facts (the input data) which need to be considered alongside the program's requirements, and which must be processed in a particular way in order to produce the output. The 'traditional' approach to the solution of the problem then takes a number of stages (represented in figure 8.1). First the programmer reaches an understanding of the problem. A solution to the problem is designed, and this solution is broken down into a series of distinct tasks. (This process is sometimes described as the development of the algorithm). The tasks required are then translated into a suitable series of programming language statements, to give the complete program.

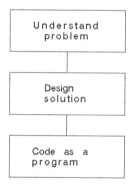

Figure 8.1 Steps in writing a program in a procedural language

The programmer working in a procedural high level language has thus understood the problem, defined a procedure to solve it and coded the necessary computer program.

The programmer working in a declarative language has a simplified task, because the language itself takes on part of the work. The tasks involved in writing a program in a declarative language such as Prolog

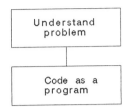

Figure 8.2 Steps in writing a program in a declarative language

are illustrated in figure 8.2. Here we see that the programmer's tasks are restricted to reaching a clear understanding of the problem, and then describing the problem to the computer using suitable language statements.

There are clear advantages to the programmer in working in a declarative language, since much of the work in writing a program is taken away from the programmer and is undertaken instead by the computer. As one might expect, there is a price to pay:

1) Efficiency:

When a programmer writes a program in a procedural language, he is able to use his intuition to define an appropriate method to use. For example, it might be that in solving a particular problem there is an obvious short cut, which can be incorporated in the solution. Similarly, more likely solutions can be selected first. When a declarative language is used to solve the same problem, the programmer is relieved from the responsibility to define the method to be used, which is instead selected by the language. Naturally the language cannot be expected to display the same intuition which the programmer might display.

We can see this sort of thing happening if we consider the problem of choosing a team of four swimmers for the ladies team from a mixed group of fifty students.

We may identify 3 levels of sophistication in making this choice.

a) The human level: If I was asked to choose four females from a large mixed group then I would expect to be able to do it reasonably successfully! I might not know exactly what had indicated to me which of the large group were male and which were female, but I would nevertheless know intuitively the sex of a reasonable proportion of the group.

b) The procedural level: A machine which attempts to solve this problem must follow a method. It does not have the benefit of intuition. But we may certainly choose to code a good, rather than bad, method. For example we could instruct the machine to select four people at random and then discard all the males and replace them with other randomly chosen students. This process could be repeated until all the four selected were female.

c) The declarative level: A machine working at this level will be given two rules. One of the rules states that four students are needed and the other states that they must all be female. The machine has no information about how to find four females in either an intuitive, or even an efficient way, but instead will apply the rules naively. Four students are selected, are they all female? If not, throw them away and find another four. Repeat this until four females are selected.

Clearly the human level provides the most 'intelligent' solution, since intuition allows an immediate acceptable team. Of the two machine solutions to the problem, the procedural one is the more sophisticated, but also provides more work for the programmer. The declarative solution might be naive and inefficient, but the machine is able to solve the problem without the programmer being required to define the method.

For a particular programming problem, we shall find that there is a straightforward trade-off between, on the one hand, the efficiency of writing the actual program (which is often far faster in a declarative language, such as Prolog) and, on the other hand, the efficiency of execution of the resulting program (where the procedural language is likely to score). The costs of software development are becoming an increasingly significant proportion of the total costs of establishing and maintaining a computer system. The costs saved by working in a declarative language, when appropriate, can be great.

2) Appropriateness:

There are some types of application in which programs written in declarative languages such as Prolog perform well, while there are other areas where declarative languages have been found to be inappropriate up to now. Application areas where Prolog is strong include the development of expert systems and other database programs, alongside logical decision-making programs, many of which are particularly difficult to write in a procedural language.

What does a Prolog program look like?

A program written in Prolog consists of a series of clauses. Each clause is of one of two types:

facts: these clauses make statements about things which are definitely and unconditionally true. They therefore correspond to statements in English such as "John is a big man" or "the sun is hot".

rules: these clauses make statements about how inferences may be drawn. For example, in English, the statement "it is a nice day if the sun is shining" is a rule. It provides us with one possible set of circumstances from which we may infer that "it is a nice day".

It is the combination of these facts and rules which enables the Prolog language to respond to goals presented by the programmer. Usually the computer is used in an interactive way.

A programming session in Prolog typically takes the form of a conversation between the programmer and the computer. The programmer will prepare a file containing a number of clauses which define the facts and rules governing a particular situation and, having loaded the file into the computer, will then present one or more goals to the computer. A goal might be a statement whose truth the computer is to test. In English, we might make the statement "It is a nice day today". If that was our Prolog goal, then the computer would be left to work through the list of clauses to see whether the facts and rules given to it did indeed lead to the conclusion that it was a nice day. The computer's response would then be true or false. Alternatively, in English we might ask the question "who is the wife of John?" and this time we would expect the Prolog system to instruct the computer to go through the clauses to find a possible solution to the problem and output the answer. This particular question might be expected to have only one solution, whereas other questions might have several answers (for example "Who is John's sister?"). Prolog systems will in any event typically find only the first solution and prompt the user as to whether to look for more.

So far we have been describing the facts, rules and goals in terms of

English statements, but although Prolog is a reasonably clear language to use, it is nevertheless necessary for the programmer to prepare the file of clauses in an appropriate form. Typically, rules and facts have the general appearance of mathematical functions, which are expressed according to a number of conventions:

:- means 'if'

so that the rule "all men are humans" might be expressed in Prolog as:

```
human(X) :- man(X).
```

The fact that "Fred is a man" might then be expressed as

```
man(fred).
```

So that a very simple set of clauses could be grouped together to form the program listed in figure 8.3.

```
man(fred).
human(X) :- man(X).
```

Figure 8.3

Notice that 'fred' has been written with a lower case f. This is done to indicate that fred is to be treated as a symbol, rather than a variable. In other words, in Prolog, any variables are given a capital letter to start their identifier, while symbols, used to represent specific individuals, will begin with a lower case character. Thus the rule 'human(X) :- man(X)' uses an upper case X to indicate that this rule applies to any man, X, rather than a particular individual, x.

If you are using a Prolog interpreter (such as ADA Educational Prolog), you will need to type these clauses into a text editor and then load them into the Prolog system. Remember to include the full stop after each clause.

Note: The command in ADA ED Prolog is

```
consult('filename').
```

To try the program out, type:

```
man(X).
```

This should result in the response

```
X = fred
```

Similarly, the goal:

```
human(X).
```

should result in the response

```
X = fred.
```

In the first case the Prolog system finds a fact to match the desired goal, while in the second case, the system combines a fact with a rule to deduce a suitable solution.

It is likely that many readers of this work will have access to the Turbo Prolog compiler. This is described as offering a 'variation of the Clocksin and Mellish Edinburgh Prolog standard'. Turbo Prolog is a compiler, which is in itself unusual since Prolog is usually implemented using an interpreter. This naturally means that the programs written in Turbo Prolog will execute more quickly than their counterparts in a corresponding interpreted version. Furthermore, Turbo Prolog provides a perfectly valid development environment for programs, but we must keep in mind the fact that it does offer a variation of the standard with which we will be most directly concerned. For this reason, alternative versions (in Turbo Prolog) will be given of some of the programs to assist the Turbo Prolog user in understanding how to run the programs discussed.

Accordingly, figure 8.4 gives a Turbo Prolog version of the earlier program given in figure 8.3.

```
domains
person = symbol
predicates
man(person)
human(person)
clauses
man(fred).
human(X) :- man(X).
```

Figure 8.4

It is evident that the Turbo Prolog version of the program is considerably longer than the standard Prolog version, but this is entirely the result of the demand by the Turbo Prolog system that all the clauses and objects used in the program are declared at the top of the program before they are used. This is presumably a condition imposed by Borland to allow for the production of a compiler environment rather than the more usual interpreter. However, other compilers do exist which do not impose this condition.

Once the Turbo Prolog version of the program is typed in (to the integral Turbo Prolog editor), it should be compiled and then run. When the program is run, the system requests that a goal should be entered. Type:

```
man(X).
```

as before and the output should be

```
X = fred
```

Next try the goal

```
human(X).
```

which should produce the output

```
X = fred
```

This is reassuring, since it indicates the fundamental similarity of the two implementations, even though in detail the instructions needed do vary.

Exercise 8.5 Include an additional fact in your Prolog program which states that 'albert' is a second man, and see whether the system which you are using can now find two humans!

Exercise 8.6 Can you add additional clauses which allow two women, Ann and Susan, to be identified as humans too?

A significant number of programs may be written using no more elaborate techniques than we have just seen. Figures 8.7 and 8.8 show an attempt at designing a simple computer-dating system. Details of the various attributes required and on offer for the members of the group are listed as clauses and rules, and the goal involves finding a suitable partner.

```
female(ann).
female(susan).
female(cheryl).
female(julie).
male(john).
male(nick).
male(mike).
male(stephen).
likes(ann,swimming).
likes(ann,popmusic).
likes(ann,walking).
likes(susan,goingout).
likes(cheryl,fastcars).
likes(julie,walking).
likes(julie,reading).
likes(john,walking).
likes(john,popmusic).
likes(nick,swimming).
likes(mike,swimming).
likes(mike,fastcars).
likes(stephen,goingout).
probablygetsonwith(X,Y) :-
        likes(X,Z),
        likes(Y,Z).
partner(X,Y) :-
        male(X),
        female(Y),
        probablygetsonwith(X,Y).
```

Figure 8.7

```
domains
person=symbol
activity=symbol
predicates
male(person)
female(person)
likes(person,activity)
probablygetsonwith(person,person)
partner(person,person)
clauses
female(ann).
female(susan).
female(cheryl).
female(julie).
male(john).
male(nick).
male(mike).
male(stephen).
likes(ann,swimming).
likes(ann,popmusic).
likes(ann,walking).
likes(susan,goingout).
likes(cheryl,fastcars).
likes(julie,walking).
likes(julie,reading).
likes(john,walking).
likes(john,popmusic).
```

```
likes(nick,swimming).
likes(mike,swimming).
likes(mike,fastcars).
likes(stephen,goingout).
probablygetsonwith(X,Y) :-
        likes(X,Z),
        likes(Y,Z).
partner(X,Y) :-
        male(X),
        female(Y),
        probablygetsonwith(X,Y).
```

Figure 8.8 The corresponding Turbo Prolog version of figure 8.7.

In order to run the programs in figures 8.7 and 8.8, you will need to give a goal such as

```
partner(X,julie).
```

or `partner(john,Y).`

This is because the partner rule as defined here is designed to take the male name first and the female name second.

Exercise 8.9 Rewrite the program above so that the partner rule takes the female name first.

Exercise 8.10 Conduct a simple survey of likes and dislikes among a mixed group of, say, twenty people, and construct a list of clauses similar to the programs in figures 8.7 and 8.8. Produce a list of suitable partners for each member in the group. (You may have some surprising results!)

Who uses Prolog?

We have already identified Prolog as being a rather different language from the others which we have discussed in this book and a glance at the programs in the previous section reveals that quite elementary programs may be written in Prolog which perform tasks which would be extremely complicated to implement in a procedural language. Readers of this book who are proficient in programming in Pascal,

BASIC or C might be interested to try to write the computer-dating program in their 'normal' programming language. The resulting code will no doubt take far longer to design and the program will be far more complex. It will presumably run more rapidly, although the delay in obtaining an answer from the Prolog system is so short as to be negligible.

The Prolog language is particularly good at solving the sort of problem that begins 'Is there any way of ...' where we are aiming to satisfy a series of conditions which can be presented naturally as a series of facts and rules. But being a good language to use for a particular task does not necessarily imply that it will be the language selected by the programmer.

Prolog has not yet become popular with the programmers who develop applications. There are several reasons for this:

1) Prolog was slow to become accepted by computer users in the USA. Although Prolog was accepted as the natural language for developing Artificial Intelligence applications in Europe from the early 1970's, LISP was the natural choice in the USA, until the point, in 1981, when the Japanese announced that their Artificial Intelligence research was to be based around the Prolog language. Therefore much of the developmental work in Prolog programming has happened only recently.

2) There is no real standard for Prolog. Although most people recognise the Clocksin and Mellish 'Edinburgh Prolog' as representing a 'standard' often implementations of the language differ from the standard in some, usually minor, ways.

3) Artificial Intelligence has been slow to become accepted. Many of the principal areas in which Prolog represents a major step forward are in the field of Artificial Intelligence, which was viewed with suspicion by many in the computer industry until comparatively recently. The result of this is that much of the work using Prolog has been done by researchers in educational institutions rather than the end-user. There has been an increase in research activity during the 1980's, some of it supported by the Alvey programme. Most commentators are agreed that the Prolog language will make significant inroads into the applications marketplace in the near future.

4) Prolog is not an easy language to learn. There is an interesting difference of opinion among the authors of introductory books which

teach the Prolog language. Some authors describe the language as 'easy' while others describe it as 'difficult'. The reason for this variation is the following: as we have already seen in this chapter, the basic ideas of Prolog are fundamentally very straightforward. It is comparatively easy to write appropriate introductory programs in Prolog and to understand what the language is succeeding in doing in order to solve the problem. On the other hand, much of the Prolog language involves the use of recursion and list processing, which the beginner finds difficult to understand fully. The beginner therefore can face severe problems in debugging programs at this point in the learning process. This problem is compounded by the fact that Prolog is a completely different type of language from the others which the programmer might already know. In earlier chapters, we have been describing languages targetted at different types of user, but we were able to identify the ways in which each language implemented common features, such as loops, if statements, and so on. A proficient procedural language programmer faced with learning to program in Prolog will find that the skills which go to make efficiency in his previous language are not identical with those which he must now employ. This is a clear disincentive to the development of applications programs in the Prolog language until it becomes more widely used.

Furthermore, we shall see that it is often the case that a Prolog program may be developed with relative ease which gives a solution to a problem, but it is frequently not a very efficient, or even an acceptable solution. For instance, in the example where we develop an expert system program in Prolog, we shall see that under certain circumstance the Prolog system will ask the same question more than once. This does not imply that it is impossible to make the program perform correctly, but does illustrate the vast increase in complexity in writing a really satisfactory program.

Despite these influences, Prolog programs have been developed with very specific purposes and used to good effect. Lucas (1988) describes several initiatives with which he has been involved in developing real working systems. One of these is the use of a Prolog program by the police to sift evidence of house burglaries within a large database of evidence. Another is the use of a Prolog program to assist with fault diagnosis in a computer network. The key factor in all of the applications described in this particular work is the use of a Prolog implementation which permits access to a relational database system. The facts used by the program become the data stored on the database, and the program becomes merely a set of rules. The actual applications are clearly similar to the traditional expert system, but the key to the success of the Prolog program in the application is the use of the existing database of facts, rather than requiring independent input of the facts into a traditional expert system package or Prolog program.

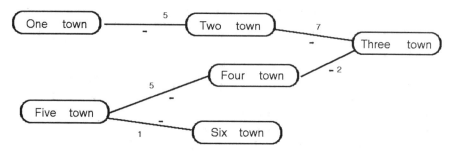

Figure 8.11 Road distances for a network of six towns

There is a list of introductory texts on Prolog in the bibliography. Unfortunately few texts currently available are able to give concrete examples based upon realistic live applications because few simple realistic applications have been developed. Many of the example programs developed take the form of language parsers, and similar esoteric applications which reflect the former nature of the language.

Prolog Applications

Example 1

In this example, we shall consider a problem known as 'network analysis'. Figure 8.11 shows a very simple network of roads linking six towns, together with the distances involved in travelling along each of the roads. The problem is to find the distance between any two towns.

As we can see from the figure, we are beginning with a very much simplified road system, in order to gain some understanding of the techniques involved, and we shall discuss later how the road system may be made more general. Take note of the arrows on the roads. These arrows denote one-way streets, which are used here in order to make our

initial programming problem simplest. A Prolog program which solves
this simplest problem is listed in figure 8.12:

```
distance(onetown,twotown,5).
distance(twotown,threetown,7).
distance(threetown,fourtown,2).
distance(fourtown,fivetown,5).
distance(fivetown,sixtown,1).
journey(X,X,0).
journey(X,Y,Z) :- distance(X,Y,Z).
journey(X,Y,Z) :-
        distance(X,W,A),
        journey(W,Y,B),
        Z = A + B.
```

Figure 8.12

Figure 8.13 lists the corresponding Turbo Prolog program:

```
  domains
town=symbol
miles=integer
  predicates
distance(town,town,miles)
journey(town,town,miles)
  clauses
distance(onetown,twotown,5).
distance(twotown,threetown,7).
distance(threetown,fourtown,2).
distance(fourtown,fivetown,5).
distance(fivetown,sixtown,1).
journey(X,X,0).
journey(X,Y,Z) :- distance(X,Y,Z).
```

```
journey(X,Y,Z) :-
      distance(X,W,A),
      journey(W,Y,B),
      Z = A + B.
```

Figure 8.13

These programs exhibit a very common technique used by Prolog programmers: recursion. Often it is easiest to define the behaviour of a relationship in terms of itself, and we see an example of this in the present example, where the rule journey() is defined in terms of itself. In order to give the total journey in miles between two arbitrary towns, we give it as the distance between the starting place and the next town, added to the journey from the new starting place to the finish (figure 8.14). Notice how the facts are listed in terms of the relation distance. The clause distance(X,Y,Z)

should be read as 'the distance from town X to town Y is Z miles. We have then defined the value of 'journey', the calculated distance between two towns, in terms of the listed values of distance and the calculated values of journey over a shorter section.

As a specific example, consider the problem of finding the total journey length between twotown and fivetown: The recursive definition of journey gives the following conclusion:

journey from twotown to fivetown equals distance from twotown to threetown plus journey from threetown to fivetown

journey from threetown to fivetown equals distance from threetown to fourtown plus journey from fourtown to fivetown

journey from fourtown to fivetown equals distance from fourtown to fivetown (which equals 5)

therefore the journey from threetown to fivetown equals (2+5)

therefore the journey from twotown to fivetown equals (7+(2+5)).

Figure 8.14

Naturally, we should like to deal with the situation where the roads are two-way, rather than one-way. We may do this by introducing additional clauses into our program as in figure 8.15.

```
distance(onetown,twotown,5).
distance(twotown,threetown,7).
distance(threetown,fourtown,2).
distance(fourtown,fivetown,5).
distance(fivetown,sixtown,1).
distance1(X,Y,Z) :- distance(X,Y,Z).
distance1(X,Y,Z) :- distance(Y,X,Z).
journey(X,X,0).
journey(X,Y,Z) :- distance1(X,Y,Z).
journey(X,Y,Z)   :- distance1(X,W,A),journey(W,Y,B),Z
= A + B.
```

Figure 8.15

It would alternatively have been possible to list each fact twice: once as the distance from A to B and once as the distance from B to A, but the method used here was chosen as being the more elegant. It has been necessary here to introduce an additional predicate 'distance1'. The reason for this is to prevent the Prolog system from entering an infinite recursive loop with a statement such as

```
distance(X,Y,Z) :- distance(Y,X,Z)
```

If this statement was encountered, the computer in determining:

```
distance(onetown,twotown,X)
```

would be prompted to consider

```
distance(twotown,onetown,X)
```

which prompts consideration of

```
distance(onetown,twotown,X)
```

and thence the infinite recursive loop. The use instead of the pre-dicate distance1() means that these definitions are not recursive and this particular infinite recursion is therefore avoided.

The Turbo Prolog version of the program from figure 8.15 is given in figure 8.16.

```
    domains
town=symbol
miles=integer
    predicates
distance(town,town,miles)
distance1(town,town,miles)
journey(town,town,miles)
    clauses
distance(onetown,twotown,5).
distance(twotown,threetown,7).
distance(threetown,fourtown,2).
distance(fourtown,fivetown,5).
distance(fivetown,sixtown,1).
distance1(X,Y,Z) :- distance(X,Y,Z).
distance1(X,Y,Z) :- distance(Y,X,Z).
journey(X,X,0).
journey(X,Y,Z) :- distance1(X,Y,Z).
journey(X,Y,Z) :-
        distance1(X,W,A),
        journey(W,Y,B),
        Z = A + B.
```

Figure 8.16.

Unfortunately, on running these programs, the user will experience only limited success. The definition of the journey predicate has been unable to prevent the possibility of passing through a particular town more than once en route. So, for example, the journey from twotown to fourtown, which has only one obvious route, has many possibilities under our definition. We might, for example, find that the computer selects the route:

```
twotown to onetown onetown to twotown twotown to
threetown threetown to fourtown.
```

The conclusion which we may draw from this, is that there are now apparently infinitely many alternative (mostly stupid) routes between any two towns. We avoided this situation before, by only allowing journeys in one direction and hence discarding all unnecessary sections of the route. Unfortunately, we will find that because of this, the Prolog system will fail to find an exhaustive list of the possible distances between any pair of points. We shall meet this situation again in the more complex road system discussed below. (This problem may be avoided by the use of the slightly more sophisticated Prolog facility: the list, see figure 8.17).

A more realistic road system is illustrated in figure 8.17 which uses various alternative routes joining pairs of towns. If we use the arrows on the diagram to represent one-way travel, then we may use a program

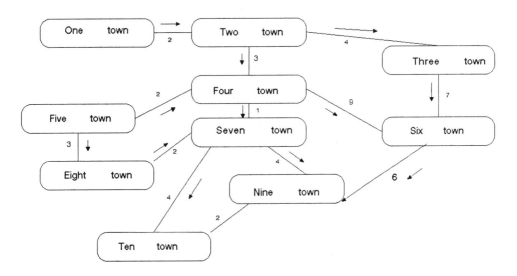

Figure 8.17 Road network for routes joining ten towns

```
   domains
place = symbol
placelist = place*
   predicates
journey(place,place,integer,placelist)
distance(place,place,integer)
member(place,placelist)
   clauses
distance(onetown,twotown,2).
distance(twotown,threetown,4).
distance(twotown,fourtown,3).
distance(fivetown,fourtown,2).
distance(threetown,sixtown,7).
distance(fourtown,sixtown,9).
distance(fourtown,seventown,1).
distance(fivetown,eighttown,3).
distance(eighttown,seventown,2).
distance(seventown,tentown,4).
distance(seventown,ninetown,4).
distance(sixtown,ninetown,6).
distance(tentown,ninetown,2).
journey(X,X,0,[]).
journey(X,Y,Z,[W|Restofroute]) :-
       distance(X,W,A),
       journey(W,Y,B,Restofroute),
       Z=A+B,
       not(member(W,Restofroute)).
```

```
member(X,[X|_]).
member(X,[_|H]) :- member(X,H).
```
Figure 8.18

like the one listed in figure 8.18.

This program uses a list variable representing the places visited en-route. The member predicate is used to check that no place is visited more than once.

Exercise 8.19 Try out the programs given here on your Prolog system. Then see whether you can produce a program for a two way system.

Exercise 8.20 See what happens if you try to find distances over the road network without maintaining a list of places already visited.

Example 2

For our second example, we shall discuss in rather more detail than before the design and specification of an Expert System package using Prolog. The approach which we shall use is broadly similar to that described in Bratko (1986). The interested reader should refer to that work for a fuller account.

Before we begin to set up the expert system, it is worth identifying exactly what constitutes an expert system.

What is an expert system?

An expert system is a computer program which behaves, within a limited domain of application, like an expert. For example, an expert system will ask a number of questions and reach a conclusion. Thus an expert system might be employed in a medical application to ask patients questions about their symptoms and to give conclusions about their likely causes.

Diagnostic systems of various types are very common forms of expert system. Expert systems have been developed for motor mechanics, telephone engineers, computer maintenance technicians as well as doctors. The theory behind all such systems is that the expert system contains the knowledge of an expert which can be obtained by a user who is not

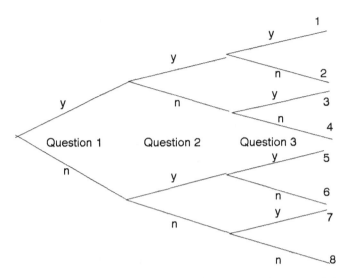

Figure 8.21   Three yes/no questions give rise to eight possible outcomes.

such an expert in the field. In theory, at least, every doctor using an expert system can give advice with the authority of the highly skilled expert whose experience and knowledge is reflected in the facts and rules in use. In practice, all expert systems are limited by:

1) The knowledge of the expert(s) who established the system

2) The size of the knowledge base which is allowed

3) The imprecise nature of the subject areas in which expert systems are set up. This is reflected in the fact that expert systems rarely give a definite diagnosis, but rather suggest a list of possible diagnoses, together with estimates of the likelihood that each possibility is correct.

The expert system may typically be thought of as constructed in three sections a) the knowledge base- which consists of the facts and rules to be used in the particular application b) the inference engine- which 'knows' how to use the information contained in the knowledge base. c) the user interface- the means of communication for the expert system user to conduct the conversation with the expert system.

The Prolog language may be used to provide both the user interface and the inference engine:

The example given below illustrates how the input/output facilities of Prolog may be used to set up the user interface. The expert system developed here is a simple diagnostic system which asks up to three (yes/no) questions about a student's performance on a course, and diagnoses the likely causes.

Figure 8.21 shows how the three questions asked give rise to eight possible outcomes. The Prolog program in figure 8.22 shows how possible outcomes are dealt with for three of the combinations of answers, and figure 8.23 shows some sample dialogues with the expert system.

```prolog
absent_of ten(X) :-
        write('Does ',X,' often miss lectures? '),
        read(Y),
        Y=yes.
works_hard(X) :-
        write('Does ',X,' hand in work on time? '),
        read(Y),
        Y=yes.
ill_often(X) :-
        write('Does ',X,' often seem ill? '),
        read(Y),
        Y=yes.
deadloss(X) :-
        absent_often(X),
        not(works_hard(X)),
        not(ill_often(X)).
unlucky(X) :-
        absent_often(X),
        works_hard(X),
        ill_often(X).
```

```
lazy(X) :-
      not(ill_often(X)),
      not(works_hard(X)),
      not(absent_often(X)).
describe(X) :-
      deadloss(X),
      write('student is a deadloss').
describe(X) :-
      unlucky(X),
      write('student is unlucky').
describe(X) :- lazy(X),
      write('student is lazy').
```

Figure 8.22

```
?- describe(fred).
Does fred often miss lectures?
yes
Does fred hand in work on time?
no
Does fred often seem ill?
no
student is a deadloss
```

Figure 8.23

One problem which we may identify while testing this program is the way in which the computer will sometimes ask a particular question more than once. We can see why this happens if we look at exactly how the Prolog system tries to satisfy its goal:

```
describe(fred).
```

The first attempt will be to try out the first possible solution:

```
describe(X) :-
    deadloss(X),
    write('deadloss').
```

In order to find out whether deadloss(fred) is satisfied, the computer will look first at absent_often(fred), then at works_hard(fred) and finally at ill_often(fred). It will stop working through the conditions as soon as it finds one which is not satisfied. Therefore, if the answers are, respectively, yes, yes, no then the output will be 'deadloss' otherwise the system will move onto the next possible combination: unlucky(X). Unlucky involves asking the same three questions, and therefore whichever questions have already been asked in trying to satisfy the deadloss() goal will be repeated in trying the unlucky() goal, and these may in their turn be repeated again in trying to satisfy the goal lazy(). The user may therefore be asked the same question repeatedly. Unfortunately, this problem is a common one in writing Prolog programs, and it is not an easy one to solve in an elegant way. The simple method involves the use of the predicate assert which allows additional facts to be added to the database as the program runs. However, many Prolog programmers consider that the user interface and inference engine should not amend the database, and therefore feel that the predicate assert is inappropriate. The interested reader is referred to one of the texts on Prolog listed in chapter 10.

Exercise 8.24 Extend the Prolog program given in figure 8.22 to include comments for all the eight possible combinations of answers to the three diagnostic questions.

Prolog's Limitations

This chapter has introduced you to a very different type of language from those discussed in the earlier chapters. As a result, in order to keep the length of the chapter reasonably short, it has not been possible to cover the full range of facilities which the Prolog language offers to the programmer. The interested reader should spend some time working through one of the many text books available which are specific to that language. We may nevertheless identify some of the limitations of the Prolog language here.

Firstly it must be clear that, just as Prolog provides a quick and easy way to solve some problems which would be much more difficult using a procedural language, other problems which procedural languages solve efficiently are correspondingly more difficult in Prolog. For example, it would be foolish to attempt to write a program which lists the first 10 integers and their squares in Prolog, since it would be so much easier to write this program in any of the procedural languages which we discussed earlier.

Secondly, the ways of thinking through a problem in a declarative language such as Prolog are rather different from those which procedural language programmers are accustomed to. There is therefore a shortfall in the number of proficient Prolog programmers. It is therefore likely that some programmers inexperienced in Prolog, will choose inappropriate methods for solving problems.

Thirdly, the learning curve in Prolog is rather steep after the initial easy introduction. This can result in programmers writing very inefficient Prolog programs rather than becoming proficient at the language.

However, it is nevertheless clear that Prolog has a very specific contribution to make in the areas where it is efficient, and to criticise it for failing to solve problems for which it was not designed is hardly fair.

9 Exercises

Introduction

In each of chapters two to eight, a programming language was described and suitable application areas identified. In a practical situation, a programmer or systems analyst would often be faced with the problem of identifying a suitable programming language for the solution of a particular programming problem. This chapter explores six realistic examples and invites the reader to consider the choice of a suitable programming language.

Questions to ask

As we have already identified, any programming problem concerns the storage and manipulation of data. Faced with a real problem, we should begin by asking ourselves:

What data is to be used within the program?

How is the data to be collected?

How is the data to be processed?

How should the data be stored to make the type of processing required convenient?

In some particular situations, the answers to one or more of these questions will eliminate some of the languages under consideration. For example, many applications really require the use of random or direct access files. This requirement immediately eliminates those languages which do not offer such a facility.

After identifying suitable languages in this way, we shall be faced with the problem of distinguishing between the alternatives. How should we do this?

1) Compatibility with existing software in use

If we have the option of using a language which is the same as that used for other software in use in the same installation, then this may well be advantageous. It will make maintenance of the various programs easier, since only one language needs to be known, and it minimises the chance that data files will be incompatible.

2) Familiarity of the programmer

It can often make sense to choose a language with which the programmer is more familiar in preference to one which is slightly more suited to the job. Programmers work more accurately and quickly in a familiar environment, and so long as the language selected can cope with the requirements of the problem, the choice of a familiar language may be justified.

3) Availability of add-on libraries

The costs of employing highly skilled programmers is far higher than the cost of buying ready-written programming libraries. The choice of a language which offers suitable libraries at reasonable cost may save time and money.

4) Characteristics of the language

We would usually aim to write well-structured programs which execute quickly. Whether we will be able to choose a language which allows this will depend upon the range of suitable languages for the particular problem.

For each of the examples presented you will need to consider the points described above alongside the characteristics of the languages which you have met. Try to put yourself in the position of a programmer/analyst faced with the problem of writing the particular program, and give a carefully reasoned discussion of suitable languages available and why you would consider a specific language most appropriate. In order to complete this task thoroughly you will need to do some casual research work to determine the range of library facilities available in the languages which you are considering. A good software catalogue will provide this information.

If you are lucky, then you will know other people using this book and you will be able to discuss your ideas about the 'correct' answers with somebody else. Do not be surprised if you come up with different answers, so long as you can justify your own position. One of the important factors which we discussed before was the programmer's previous experience and expertise, and this could account for different choices by different people.

Example 1 Company Payroll

The traditional company payroll system uses sequential file processing based upon a master file containing data in a form such as that shown in figure 9.1.

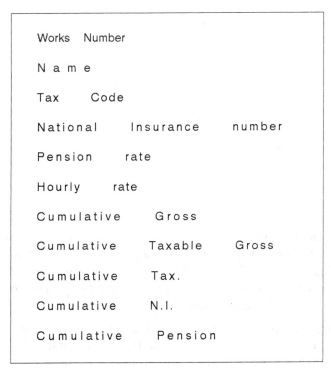

Works   Number

N a m e

Tax   Code

National   Insurance   number

Pension   rate

Hourly   rate

Cumulative   Gross

Cumulative   Taxable   Gross

Cumulative   Tax.

Cumulative   N.I.

Cumulative   Pension

Figure 9.1

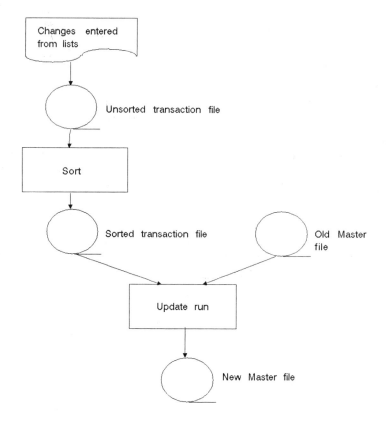

Figure 9.2

Each time the payroll application is to be run, the masterfile must first be updated to show details of any changes in staff (as shown in the flowchart in figure 9.2) before combining the masterfile with details of sickness and overtime for the current period to produce payslips and a new masterfile with updated subtotals (figure 9.3).

The tendency has been for payroll systems to be implemented using COBOL. If you were employed to specify the language for a new payroll system of this type, then what would be your choice?

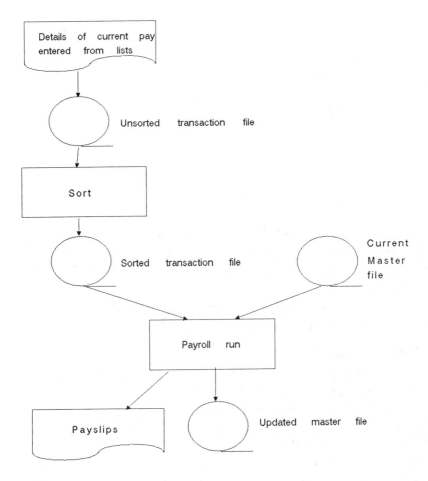

Figure 9.3

Example 2 Personnel Records System

Many company computer systems now integrate the payroll system within a wider system dealing with all personnel matters, including the payroll. These more sophisticated systems need direct as well as sequential access to files, since it is necessary to be able to update the personnel records on a particular employee at any time, to ensure, for example, that the emergency contact address on the computer record is always up-to-date.

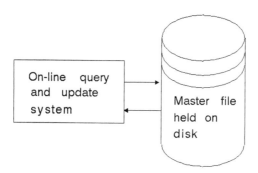

Figure 9.4

We are therefore faced with a system which requires the same sequential access to the data as described in example 1, but has the additional requirement of the direct access query and updating of personnel records. (Figure 9.4).

Once again, these systems are typically implemented using COBOL. Do you think that this would be your choice?

Example 3 Mailing List

A small business wishes to use a computer to set up a mailing list of names and addresses of customers from which suitable customers may be selected and name and address labels produced. On the assumption that the software is to be written specially for this user, consider which programming languages might be suitable.

Applications such as this one lend themselves to the production of standard applications packages which may be purchased already written. Investigate in software catalogues what facilities are offered by some of the available packages. If possible, try to find out what language the programs are written in (This information may not be readily available).

Many packages of this type would be developed using BASIC on a microcomputer. To what extent would you criticise this choice of language?

Example 4 Health analysis

A program is required to analyse lifestyle and make observations and recommendations for changes which will lead to a more healthy life. In this situation, an interactive program will be required which will ask the user a series of questions and react according to the answers. There will be a database of information which relates various possible answers, and combinations of answers, to a particular health risk. The program will print out an appropriate piece of advice chosen from those available.

A number of programs have been developed using techniques such as these, and they have almost always been based upon traditional procedural languages- and often BASIC, which makes the writing of simple interactive programs particularly straightforward. Would you agree that this approach is appropriate?

Example 5 Health testing

A natural extension to the ideas used in example 4 apply in health testing programs, which use specially designed monitoring equipment to allow various data to be collected directly from a person exercising and be input to the computer and analysed immediately.

Naturally, the automatic data entry in such a system is attractive. The only difficulty attached to this addition to the program is the need to have interfacing directly with the external devices which may imply a need for low-level programming or at least support for low-level routines within a high-level program. How does this affect your choice of language.

Example 6 Scientific data analysis

A scientific experiment is to be controlled and monitored by computer using a data-logging system. In this system, various data are collected at fixed time points and input directly to the computer. They are to be stored in a database for subsequent on-line query and sophisticated numerical calculations.

This is a fairly typical situation within a research environment. The requirement to collect data directly from an experiment seems to imply the selection of a language which offers low-level support. On the other hand, the maintenance of an on-line enquiry system suggests the need for file handling of some complexity. Finally, the complex numerical calculations would traditionally be carried out for scientists by using a language such as FORTRAN, which would be unsuitable for the file-handling operations.

Try to examine the languages indicated by the separate sections of
this problem, and identify those which would be totally unable to
complete other sections. This should leave a list of languages which
could plausibly be used for the whole program. Can you think of any
better alternatives to this?

Epilogue

To program or not to program.

There is a body of opinion, which has become increasingly wide-spread recently, that programming is out of date, and that software packages are available off the shelf to solve almost all applications problems today. For some applications this is true, while for others it is still necessary to write programs more or less from scratch because there has been no previous work in the particular area. In between these two extremes lie various possibilities.

One possibility is the use of special library facilities as we have described alongside many of the available languages.

Another common option is the use of a highly specialised package which can be configured to suit various applications with similar data processing requirements. Probably the best known type of package is the database. Here a package is offered which allows for the storage and manipulation of a database in different ways. Typically the database is configured by writing a 'program' in the database 'language'.

Program generators have appeared from time to time. These are packages which allow the user to specify details of the problem and the processing requirements and then purport to write the program in a suitable language. Packages like this are highly attractive, but often disappointing in the performance of the programs. Sometimes they are excessively restrictive in the appications which they can support, others may produce rather inefficient code. Nevertheless these Computer Assisted Software Engineering (CASE) tools are exciting, because they are likely to become increasingly significant in the production of programs as hardware and software develops.

Object Oriented Programming (OOP) has recently become available. The programmer is offered the facility to describe a problem in terms of 'objects'. Objects provide a way of combining characteristics and operations to give a level of abstraction beyond that offered by records and procedures. Turbo Pascal version 5.5 and C++ both offer these facilities.

All of these tools and approaches are beyond the scope of the present volume, and the interested reader is referred to books on particular packages. It is, however, interesting to note that alongside the growth in the use of these specialised tools to assist in the quick development of programs has been a parallel increase in the demand for programmers experienced in software development through traditional high-level programming. Indeed applications are frequently prototyped using CASE tools before being re-coded, in final form, directly in high-level language.

Where to from here?

I hope that you have found some interesting material in this book and that it will have encouraged you to want to know more. Perhaps you are now able to select a new language to learn, or perhaps you have become convinced that your present skills are sufficient. The bibliography lists books specific to the separate languages described here.

Bibliography

This bibliography lists those books referred to explicitly in the text, alongside other books available on specific languages which are recommended for further reading. For simplicity, the books are subdivided according to the language which they cover, and a section of general books is also included. The list is not intended to be exhaustive, but to provide a starting point for those readers who do not have an extensive reference library available to them.

General books on Programming Languages

Mayer H.G. (1988) *Programming Languages*, Macmillan

Terry P.D. (1986) *Programming Language Translation*, Addison Wesley

Wilson L.B. and Clark R.G. (1988) *Comparative Programming Languages*, Addison Wesley.

BASIC

Alcock D. (1986) *Illustrating BASIC,* CUP.

Ford N.J. (1990, to appear) *BASIC Applications: A first course in structured programming,* NCC Blackwell.

Howard M.L. (1987) *Understanding and Using Microsoft BASIC/IBM PC BASIC,* West Publishing Co.

Pascal

Bishop J. (1989) *Pascal Precisely* (2nd Ed), Addison Wesley.

Brown P.J. (1982) *Pascal from BASIC*, Addison Wesley

Findlay W. and Watt D.A. (1985) *Pascal: An introduction to methodical programming* (3rd Ed), Pitman.

Ford J. (1990, to appear) *Pascal by Example*, NCC Blackwell.

Holmes B.J. (1987) *Pascal Programming,* DP Publications.

Jensen K. and Wirth N. (1975) *Pascal- User Manual and Report,* Springer-Verlag.

COBOL

Ellis Computing (1987) *Utah COBOL 4.0,* Ellis Computing.

Holmes B.J. (1986) *Structured Programming in COBOL* (2nd Ed), DP Publications.

Parkin A. (1975) *COBOL for Students,* Edward Arnold.

FORTRAN

Chivers I. and Clark M. (1984) *Interactive FORTRAN 77,* Ellis Horwood.

Ellis T.M.R. (1980) *Structured FORTRAN ,* University of Sheffield.

Metcalf M. (1985) *Effective FORTRAN 77,* OUP.

C

Banahan M. (1988) *The C Book,* Addison-Wesley.

Berry R.E., Meekings B.A.E. and Soren M.D. (1988) *A Book on C* (2nd Ed), Macmillan.

Kernighan B.W. and Ritchie D.M. (1978) *The C Programming language,* Prentice Hall.

Waite M., Prata S. and Martin D. (1987) *C Primer Plus,* H.W. Sams and Co.

Modula-2

Knepley E. and Platt R. (1985) *Modula-2 Programming,* Prentice-Hall.

Sale A. (1986) *Modula-2 Discipline and Design,* Addison-Wesley.

Schildt H. (1987) *Advanced Modula-2,* Osborne McGraw-Hill.

Wirth N. (1982) *Programming in Modula-2,* Springer-Verlag

Prolog

Bratko I. (1986) *Prolog Programming for Artificial Intelligence,* Addison-Wesley.

Clocksin W.F. and Mellish C.S. (1987) *Programming in Prolog* (3rd Ed), Springer-Verlag.

Doores J., Reiblein A.R. and Vadera S. (1987) *Prolog-Programming for Tomorrow,* Sigma.

Lucas R. (1988) *Database Applications Using Prolog,* Ellis Horwood.

Rogers J.B. (1987) *A Turbo Prolog Primer,* Addison-Wesley.

Language Implementations

There follows a list of the principal programming language implementations which have been used in the example programs given in the text. Where an alternative implementation has been used for a particular example, this fact appears within the text.

BASIC:

1. *RM Basic Version 2.0,* on a RM Nimbus PC.

2. *Borland Turbo BASIC Version 1.1* on an IBM PC XT Compatible.

Pascal:

Borland Turbo Pascal Version 5.5 on an IBM PC XT Compatible.

COBOL:

Ellis Computing Utah COBOL Version 4.0 on an IBM PC XT Compatible.

FORTRAN:

Fortransoft FS FORTRAN 77 Version 3.16 on an IBM PC XT Compatible.

Modula-2:

JPI Topspeed Modula-2 Version 1.15 on an IBM PC XT Compatible.

Prolog:

1. *ADA Educational Prolog Version 1.95D* on an IBM PC XT Compatible.

2. *Borland Turbo Prolog Version 1.1* on an IBM PC XT Compatible.

C Library:

The Window Boss by P. Mongelluzo, Star Guidance Consulting Inc., 273 Windy Drive, Waterbury, Connecticut, O6705, USA. y

INDEX

accumulator 3

ADA 173,193

Algol 60 53

algorithmic language 201

ALLOCATE 182

Alvey 212

Animals 70

ANSI 80,114,139

artificial intelligence 201

assembler 4,6

assembly language 4

B 137

Bell laboratories 137

binary 3

block-structured 53

Borland 57

C 193

C++ 235

CASE 235

clause 205

COBOL 193

CODASYL 79

compiler 6,11,12

complex 117

concurrency 173,190

conformant array parameters 184

coprocesses 191

CP/M 57

database 234

DBase 91

declaration 33

declarative language 201

definition module 186

DIVISION 82

double precision 117

editor 11

education 25

expert system 201,221

factorial 69

file 57,158

FORTRAN 193

graphics 25

health analysis 232

health testing 233

hosted C implementation 141

IBM PC 57

implementation 13,56

implementation module 186

IMPORT 175

instructions 3

integrated development environment 11

interpreter 6,11,12

interrupt 193

language- high level 5

language- low level 5

library 13,139,153,228,234

link 12

LINT 186

LISP 212

log in 10

loop 7,53

machine code 4

macro 4,147

mailing list 232

matrix 126

memory allocation 7

menu 26

MERGE 89

mnemonic 4

module 172

music 25

NAG 115

Newton's method 132

number crunching 81

numerical analysis 130

object code 12

OOP 235

open array parameters 184

operating system 10,19

overlays 12

Pascal 171,193

payroll 229

personnel records 230

pointer 154

portable 13,50,171

preprocessor 143

procedural language 201

program 4

program generators 234

program modula 186

QuickSort 198

recursion 69

Report Writer 89

scientific data analysis 233

shareware 164

shift 166

sorting 87

source code 12

spaghetti 134

SQL 91

strongly typed 53

structure 22,50

text file 78

toast 190

TopSpeed Modula-2 196

translation 4,6

Turbo Basic 24

Turbo C 159

Turbo Pascal 13,57,235

Turbo Prolog 207

UNIX 137

vector 126

Window BOSS 164

Wirth 49,171

Zortech C 159

ELLIS HORWOOD SERIES IN COMPUTERS AND THEIR APPLICATIONS

Series Editor: IAN CHIVERS, Consultant to the Monitoring and Assessment Research Centre, London, and formerly Senior Programmer and Analyst, Imperial College of Science and Technology, University of London

Rubin, T.	USER INTERFACE DESIGN FOR COMPUTER SYSTEMS
Rudd, A.S.	PRACTICAL USAGE OF ISPF DIALOG MANAGER
de Saram, H.	PROGRAMMING IN MICRO-PROLOG
Savic, D. & Goodsell, D.	APPLICATIONS PROGRAMMING WITH SMALLTALK/V
Schirmer, C.	PROGRAMMING IN C FOR UNIX
Schofield, C.F.	OPTIMIZING FORTRAN PROGRAMS
Sharp, J.A.	DATA FLOW COMPUTING
Sherif, M.A.	DATABASE PROJECTS
Smith & Sage	EDUCATION AND THE INFORMATION SOCIETY
Smith, J.M & Stutely, R.	SGML
Späth, H.	CLUSTER ANALYSIS ALGORITHMS
Späth, H.	CLUSTER DISECTION AND ANALYSIS
Stratford-Collins, P.	ADA
Tizzard, K.	C FOR PROFESSIONAL PROGRAMMERS
Turner, S.J.	AN INTRODUCTION TO COMPILER DESIGN
Wexler, J.	CONCURRENT PROGRAMMING IN OCCAM 2
Whiddett, R.J.	CONCURRENT PROGRAMMING FOR SOFTWARE ENGINEERS
Whiddett, R.J., Berry, R.E., Blair, G.S., Hurley, P.N., Nicol, P.J., Muir, S.J.	UNIX
Yannakoudakis, E.J. & Hutton, P.J.	SPEECH SYNTHESIS AND RECOGNITION SYSTEMS
Zech, R.	FORTH

Computer Communications and Networking

Currie, W.S.	LANS EXPLAINED
Deasington, R.J.	A PRACTICAL GUIDE TO COMPUTER COMMUNICATIONS AND NETWORKING, 2nd Edition
Deasington, R.J.	X.25 EXPLAINED, 2nd Edition
Henshall, J. & Shaw, S.	OSI EXPLAINED
Kauffels, F.-J.	PRACTICAL LANS ANALYSED
Kauffels, F.-J.	PRACTICAL NETWORKS ANALYSED
Kauffels, F.-J.	UNDERSTANDING DATA COMMUNICATIONS
Muftic, S.	SECURITY MECHANISMS FOR COMPUTER NETWORKS